CLEAN
YOUR WAY TO HAPPY

CLEAN

YOUR WAY TO HAPPY

Alexandra Fraser

Originally published in Great Britain in 1999
as Trade Secrets: Cleaning by Orion Books Ltd
This edition first published in 2019 by Orion Spring
an imprint of The Orion Publishing Group Ltd
Carmelite House, 50 Victoria Embankment
London EC4Y 0DZ

An Hachette UK Company

10 9 8 7 6 5 4 3 2 1

A CIP catalogue record for this book is
available from the British Library.

ISBN (Trade paperback) 978 1 8418 8352 6

Printed in Great Britain by Clays Ltd, Elcograf S.p.A

MIX
Paper from
responsible sources
FSC® C104740

www.orionbooks.co.uk

Contents

Foreword

'Here lies a poor woman who was always tired
For she lived in a place where help wasn't hired.
Her last words on earth were, 'Dear Friends,
    I am going
Where washing ain't done nor sweeping nor
    sewing
And everything there is exact to my wishes
For there they don't eat and there's no washing
    of dishes...
Don't mourn for me now, don't mourn for me ever
For I'm going to do nothing for ever and ever...'
Anonymous Epitaph

Forgive us for claiming that this book
might be a lifesaver, but perhaps if this
poor woman had had a copy, her days on
this earth might have been, if not prolonged,
at least a little more enjoyable.

It is an inescapable fact of life that we all
have to clean – whether ourselves, our
homes, our clothes or our possessions. For
the true cleaning perfectionist, this book

contains hundreds of suggestions to help achieve shiny shoes, flawless floors and beatific bathrooms.

For the rest of us, however, the charm of these tips lie in their ability to make life easier. Many save time, most save money and hopefully all should save us from working ourselves into the ground.

KITCHENS

. . . .

'Tis by cleanliness a cook must please.'
William King

Ovens

....

'Everything's getting on top of me.
I can't switch off. I've got a self-cleaning
oven – I have to get up in the night to see
if it's doing it.'
Victoria Wood

Messy ovens needn't take hours to clean.
> A sheet of aluminium foil on the bottom
> will catch all the drips and spills. Replace
> as necessary.

To clean up any spills in the oven,
> sprinkle some salt and cinnamon over
> the spill. This stops the house from
> filling with that acrid smoky smell and
> the spill will be easy to lift off with a
> spatula.

Or sprinkle with automatic dish-washing powder,
> cover with wet paper towels, let stand
> for a few hours, then clean with a damp
> sponge.

Keep salt near the cooker to avoid a grease fire.

Following a spill, immediately sprinkle with the salt. When the oven cools, brush off, then wipe with a damp sponge.

Forget specialist oven cleaners. For an inexpensive alternative

that will remove even hard, baked-on grease put your oven on warm for about two minutes, then turn it off. Place a small dish of full-strength household ammonia on the top shelf and a large pan of boiling water on the bottom shelf and leave overnight. In the morning, open the oven and air for a while before washing down with soapy water.

Another way to avoid using toxic oven cleaners...

Sprinkle the oven with water and bicarbonate of soda then start scrubbing. This also works well on baths.

To clean your hob,

try white vinegar. Not only does it bring up a nice shine, but it will eliminate persistent cooking smells too.

To keep the kitchen smelling sweet,
put some orange peel in the oven
(at 350°F/ 180°C/ Gas Mark 4).

Alternatively,
if the pong is really strong, boil a dozen
cloves in a mixture of one cup of water
and a quarter cup of vinegar.

Clean a grotty roasting tin
(not aluminium or non-stick) with a
solution of washing soda and water
boiled up in the tin. Rinse and then dry
in a cool oven.

Cleaning a greasy grill pan
is a horrible job. Line your grill pan with
foil beneath the wire tray and simply lift
the foil out – complete with dirt and fat –
after use.

Don't try to keep your baking tins
shining like new – once they are matt
and dark they will actually retain the
heat much better!

Appliances

'All the modern inconveniences'
Mark Twain

To rid white appliances of yellowing,
mix together one half cup of bleach, one
quarter cup of baking soda and four cups
of warm water. Apply with a sponge
and leave for ten minutes. Rinse and dry
thoroughly. Sparkling white!

Wipe large items like freezers and washing machines with car wax
to make them shine and to remove small
scratches.

If your microwave needs a good clean,
add two tablespoons of either lemon
juice or baking soda to a cup of water in
a large microwave-safe container. Let the
mixture boil for four to six minutes in
the microwave, then wipe the walls and
door clean with a sponge or cloth.

Although microwaves hardly need cleaning,
just remember to wipe them over with a
damp cloth immediately after each use.

Use rubbing alcohol
instead of expensive commercial waxes
on all white goods.

Dishwashers will work just as effectively
if you use the cheapest brand of dish-
washing detergent available but add
a few tablespoons of vinegar to the
detergent. The vinegar will cut the
grease, leave your dishes sparkling and
save you some pennies.

Remove smelly fridge odours,
by filling a small bowl with charcoal and
placing it on a shelf in the refrigerator.

**Also, an open box of baking soda
will absorb odours**
for at least a month or two.

For a truly sweet smelling fridge,

> pour vanilla extract onto a piece of cotton wool and leave it on one of the shelves.

Keep the coils at the back of your fridge clean.

> Unplug and pull out the fridge regularly and use your vacuum cleaner to remove dust and dirt. The fridge will stay efficient and last longer too.

To clean underneath the refrigerator,

> tie a sock around the end of a stick or broom handle.

To prevent the sticky film on dishes and the inside of the dishwasher,

> put a bowl containing one cup of bleach in the bottom of the empty dishwasher. Run through the wash cycle but do not dry. Then fill the bowl with one cup of white vinegar and run through an entire cycle.

To clean your dish-washer,
>put a cup of white vinegar at the bottom of your empty dishwasher and run it through the entire cycle.

General

'Old ways are the safest and surest ways.'
Sir Edward Coke

Rubber spatula ready for the bin?
>Trim off the tattered edges and keep trimming until there's nothing left!

Spray vegetable oil on a grater
>before use for a fast clean-up.

To clean a grater,
>after use, rub a hard crust of bread over it.

Graters are impossible to clean
>without losing a bit of your finger ... an old toothbrush does the trick and is ideal for sieves as well.

Use baking soda
to remove coffee and tea stains from
plastic cups and dishes.

**Plastic bread wrappers often melt onto the
side of toasters**
– to remove this, rub nail-varnish
remover on to the melted bit and rub it
off with a cloth.

To get rid of odours from plastic containers,
fill with crumpled-up black and white
newspaper. Cover tightly and leave
overnight. Next day the smell will
be gone.

**And to get rid of the strong plastic smell from
new containers,**
wash, dry and put in the freezer for at
least two days.

If your waste disposal has bad breath,
try feeding it a handful of ice cubes, a
splash of vinegar, a whole lemon and a
pinch of allspice.

Never put celery or other stringy matter in the waste disposal unit.

Drop fresh parsley into hot oil after use to absorb unwanted flavours.
The oil can then be reused without affecting the taste of the next food to be cooked.

To remove limescale in a kettle,
fill with equal parts of vinegar and water. Bring to the boil and allow to stand overnight. Rinse thoroughly.

No need to use abrasive cleaners for counter tops,
wash them daily with a solution of mild dish-washing liquid and water to keep them clean.

Keep your knives gleaming and rust-free
– plunge them into an onion and leave there for half an hour. Wash and then polish lightly with some vegetable oil.

Also, keep a good knife clean
by dipping a cork in scouring powder
and running it along the side of the blade.
Rinse the knife, dry it and wipe it down
with vegetable oil.

Rotate your best cutlery.
Take it from the left-hand side of the
drawer and put it back on the right-
hand side.

Be careful when washing silver cutlery.
Take care it doesn't rub together too
much. Silver is a soft metal and picks up
scratches easily.

Boiled eggs will turn metal cutlery black
if left on. Always clean your spoon
immediately after eating eggs!

Clean a copper kettle
by covering it with brown sauce and
leaving overnight. Wash the sauce off
next morning and admire your reflection
in the shiny surface!

If your hands smell of onions,
soak them in some milk.

Cabbage can stink when it's being cooked.
A bay leaf added to the boiling water will stop the smell without affecting the taste of the vegetable.

To stop your bins from smelling unpleasant,
throw a few fresh herbs in each time you throw something away.

Keep swing-bin liners in the bottom of your bin.
When you take out a full bag, a new liner will always be at hand.

When you wash the kitchen floor,
use your rubbish bin instead of a bucket to hold the water. This way you get a fresh bin without the extra job of washing it.

Dropped an egg on the kitchen floor?
Add some salt to the egg, leave it for five minutes and it will clean up more easily.

Sterilize your kitchen cloths
> by popping them newly washed into the microwave and 'cooking' them on high for a few minutes.

Clean your thermos flask
> by adding a few tablespoons of baking soda and filling with warm water. Let it stand, then rinse thoroughly.

Pots and Pans

'If ifs and ands were pots and pans there'd be no work for tinkers.'
Thomas Love Peacock

If you're cooking a big casserole,
> put a sheet of tin foil between the pot and the lid to save having to wash the grimy lid afterwards.

To clean burnt and scorched pans,

sprinkle liberally with baking soda and moisten with water. After standing for several hours, you can generally lift the burned portions out of the pan.

Remove stubborn stains from non-stick cookware

by boiling two tablespoons of baking soda with half a cup of vinegar and one cup of water for ten minutes. Before using, season the pan with vegetable or sunflower oil.

For sparkling copper pots,

fill a spray bottle with vinegar and add three tablespoons of salt. Then spray the solution onto the copper pot. Allow to stand for one hour and then rub clean.

Tarnish troubles?

Rub on Worcestershire sauce and they will disappear.

Or,

try dipping lemon halves in salt and rubbing.

Don't despair if you burn a frying pan.
>Boil up some sliced onions and water in the pan and leave for several hours.

Alternatively,
>you could boil up some water and vinegar in a burnt pan and leave it overnight. It will be easier to clean in the morning.

Or, if disaster strikes and you really burn a pan,
>leave some cold tea to soak in the pan for a few hours. The black burnt-in crust will then come away quite easily.

Likewise, to clean a pan after cooking smelly fish,
>leave some strong cold tea in the pan for ten minutes before you come to wash it. No lingering smells!

Also,
>vinegar in the washing-up water will remove the fishy smell from pots and pans.

To remove a fishy smell from hands,
rinse them in lemon juice.

To clean badly burnt saucepans,
soak in cola for a while.

To clean an aluminium pan,
boil the peel of an apple in some water.
This will make it much easier to clean
the pan afterwards.

If you have a discoloured aluminium pan,
add a few sticks of rhubarb or a couple of
tomatoes. Boil up with plenty of water
and the food acids will lift the stain.

To clean copper-bottomed pans,
sprinkle with salt and rub with half a
lemon.

**To clean really baked-on food from a cooking
pan,**
put a sheet of fabric conditioner in the
pan and fill with water. Leave overnight
and the next day the food will just lift off
with a sponge.

Clean cast-iron skillets
on the outside with a commercial oven
cleaner. Let stand for two hours. Then
remove any accumulated black stains
with vinegar and water.

Sinks

....

*'The sink is the great symbol of the
bloodiness of family life.'*
Julian Mitchell

When disinfecting your sink,
don't bother with strong chemical
solutions. Just use ordinary household
salt.

**Baking soda is excellent for cleaning
stainless-steel sinks.**

To give a stainless-steel sink a superb finish,
rub it down with a scrunched up ball of
newspaper after cleaning.

To remove water spots from a stainless-steel sink,

use a cloth dampened with rubbing alcohol or white vinegar.

Rub stainless-steel sinks with lighter fluid if rust marks appear.

After the rust disappears, wipe with your regular kitchen cleaner.

To remove hard water lime deposits from your stainless-steel draining board,

soak in full strength white vinegar, then scrub.

For a sparkling white sink,

bleach is best. It is expensive to fill a basin with bleach though, so, line it first with kitchen paper towels, then soak the paper in bleach. Leave for an hour or so before throwing the paper away.

Never use bleach in a coloured porcelain sink

because it will fade the colour. Instead, clean with mild liquid detergents, vinegar or baking soda.

Don't put kitchen fat down the sink
– let it solidify in a container, like a yoghurt pot, and then put it in the bin.

To rid your sink of soap suds after washing up,
wipe around the sink with a bar of soap while the tap is running.

Glass and China

'There's a joy without canker or cark,
There's a pleasure eternally new,
'Tis to gloat on the glaze and the mark,
Of China that's ancient and blue.'
Andrew Lang

Water down your glass cleaner to make it go further.
It will work just as effectively.

To clean a gilded ceramic plate,
simply soak it overnight in fabric conditioner and water. If there is no gilding, then soak in a weak bleach solution.

To get rid of unsightly build-up in the bottom of a vase,
add a few drops of automatic dish-washer detergent and fill with hot water. Soak overnight, then rinse.

To remove tea or coffee stains from fine china,
rub with a damp cloth dipped in baking soda.

If you're washing china by hand,
add vinegar to the rinse water for a cleaner and brighter shine.

Likewise, a little vinegar added to the final rinse
will leave glasses sparkling.

When washing crystal,
rinse in one part vinegar to three parts warm water and air dry – preferably outside in bright sunshine.

If you must dry the glassware immediately,
newspaper brings out a shine, but use newspaper that is at least two days old, because the ink will come off new papers.

To dry a decanter,
use a hair-dryer on a medium setting.

Here's something to smile about: good quality china will really sparkle
if soaked with denture-cleaning tablets!

If your decanter looks stained or dull,
fill it with vinegar and crushed eggshells. Replace the stopper and give it a good hard swill round. Once rinsed with warm water, it will look as good as new.

Alternatively,
half fill the decanter with warm soapy water and two tablespoons of rice. Swish the mixture round and after half an hour remove the solution. Rinse the decanter and stand upside down to dry.

To pack glassware for a move,
wrap wet newspaper around the glass and let it dry. It will act like a cast around the glass.

Save water when doing the dishes

– use a washing-up bowl rather than
filling a whole sink.

Also, don't rinse dishes under a running hot water tap

– have a second bowl of clean water
standing by instead.

And,

you can always use this rinsing water for
the garden afterwards.

Polish delicate glasses with a soft, dry cloth,

not a damp one, which will grip the
glasses and possibly break them.

Never store glasses upside down.

They will absorb the smells of the
cupboard that they've been kept in and
this could affect the taste of the wine.

Don't worry about glasses collecting dust

if you store them upright. Glasses should
be cleaned before use anyway.

Keep your teapots smelling fresh
– put a sugar lump or dry tea bag inside until you want to use it.

Never put a delicate glass into hot water bottom side first,
it will crack from sudden expansion. The most delicate glassware will be safe if it is slipped in sideways.

When washing delicate crystal or glasses,
first line the bottom of the sink with a towel or terry nappy.

When two glasses are stuck together,
fill the top one with cold water and slowly dip the bottom one into hot water.

Scratches in glassware will disappear if polished with toothpaste.

If you don't have a bottle brush,
half fill a vase or bottle with warm soapy water and a handful of fine gravel. Shake vigorously. If the glass is delicate, replace the gravel with split-peas or dried lentils.

To clean a smelly vase or glass,
half fill it with water and add a
tablespoon of mustard. Shake the
mixture and then leave for an hour
before rinsing thoroughly.

To clean a narrow-necked vase,
fill with water and pop in a couple of
denture-cleaning tablets.

Chopping Boards

'The Microbe is so very small
You cannot make him out at all ...'
Hilaire Belloc

To clean and deodorize wooden boards,
combine half a cup of baking soda with
some warm water to make a paste. Rub
the paste on to the wood. Rinse well
with clear water and pat dry.

To restore the wood sheen,
rub in salad oil or linseed oil using a fine
steel-wool pad.

Alternatively,
clean wooden chopping boards with half
a lemon dipped in salt. This also prevents
the surface from staining.

To clear fish guts and scales
from your chopping board, use a window
squeegee.

Or, ideally, clean fish on newspaper instead;
this keeps your board clean and means
you can wrap the waste up and put it
straight into the bin.

Mustard removes fishy smells
from wooden boards.

**To remove strong food smells from plastic
chopping boards,**
give them a rub down with a cut
grapefruit.

Always dry wooden chopping boards upright
and not flat to stop them from warping.

BATHROOMS

....

'Go, and never darken my towels again.'
Groucho Marx

Showers

....

'This is our finest shower.'
John Osborne

Glass shower doors will stay cleaner longer
    if you spray them lightly with furniture
    polish, and then shine.

To wash shower curtains,
    put them in the washing-machine along
    with one large bath towel. Add half a cup
    each of detergent and baking soda. Then
    select a warm wash, adding one cup of
    white vinegar to the rinse cycle. Do not
    spin dry or wash the vinegar out. Hang
    immediately and wrinkles will disappear
    when completely dry.

Shower curtains
    (plastic or polyester) with mildew spots
    should be soaked in a solution of one
    part domestic bleach to four parts water.
    Then rinse thoroughly or machine wash
    if possible.

Grimy shower curtains

should be wiped with distilled vinegar, then rinsed with water.

Get rid of soap scum from shower doors

by rubbing with a used sheet of fabric conditioner.

To stop the bottom of your shower curtain from becoming discoloured or mouldy

coat it with baby oil.

If your shower head is clogged

fill a plastic freezer bag with about 2 in/ 5 cm of vinegar and place the shower head in the bag. Wrap a tie wrap or elastic band around the neck of the shower head to hold the bag in place. Leave in place overnight. In the morning remove the bag and the head should be clean and function properly. Repeat if necessary.

Glass shower doors

quickly look grubby and limescale
can be hard work to get rid of. Try using
a squeegee – the sort motoring shops
sell for car windscreens – for a sparkling
look in minutes!

To clean glass shower doors

try using left-over white wine.

Deep clean shower surrounds

using a sponge mop dipped in a solution
of half a cup of vinegar, one cup of
household ammonia and a quarter cup
of baking soda in 1 gallon/4.5 litres of
warm water. Make sure you don a pair
of rubber gloves before you begin. After
cleaning, rinse with warm water.

Remove water spots on metal frames

around shower doors and enclosures with
lemon oil furniture polish – on page 83
you'll find the recipe.

A toothbrush and toothpaste works wonders on shower door runners.

Make your own spray cleaner
by adding three tablespoons of household ammonia and one tablespoon of vinegar to a spray bottle and filling to the top with cool water.

Baths

'Bath twice a day to be really clean, once a day to be passably clean, once a week to avoid being a public menace.'
Anthony Burgess

To clean a bath
use an old net curtain. It's mildly abrasive and gets the marks off brilliantly.

Alternatively,
to clean delicate surfaces, sheer tights make an excellent, non-abrasive scouring pad.

Bathroom tile grout a bit grotty?
Simply camouflage with some correction fluid.

Always wipe the bath down after use.
Some essential oils can mark plastic baths if they are left on the surface.

Avoid hard-to-remove tide marks on the bath
– don't use concentrated bath oils.

When descaling tap nozzles,
put a plastic bag filled with vinegar over the nozzle. Secure it with an elastic band and leave it for at least half an hour.

Shift hard water deposits from around the base of taps
with an old toothbrush dipped in vinegar. Rinse well afterwards.

Mould spots on bath sealant
should be tackled with domestic bleach and a toothbrush. Rinse thoroughly.

Toilets

....

'Plunge it in the depths: it comes up more beautiful.'
Horace

Keep your toilet bowl looking clean
– just put ½pint/150 ml of white vinegar in the bowl for about five minutes and then flush.

To clean out a blocked loo pan,
use an old string mop. A couple of plunges should do the trick.

To clean a filthy toilet bowl,
pour a can of fizzy cola around the rim. Leave it for an hour and then brush and flush!

Alternatively,
to clean a loo, drop several denture-cleaning tablets into the toilet bowl.

To remove toilet rings,
flush first to wet sides and apply a paste
of borax and lemon juice. Let sit for two
hours, then scrub.

Safety first
– never use two different commercial
cleaners in the loo at the same time –
they may combine to produce dangerous
gases or even explode!

To clean a really grubby toilet,
tie a cloth around a toilet brush, plunge
vigorously and push the water down
the u-bend and out of the toilet. Then
soak the bowl in bleach for several hours
before reflushing.

Alternatively,
rub with a fine grade sandpaper (wet the
sandpaper if the dirty rings are very old).

When bleaching your toilet,
don't forget to put some bleach into the
toilet-brush holder to ensure the brush
stays clean.

General

....

'Martin, if dirt were trumps, what hands you would hold.'
Charles Lamb

To clear a blockage in a sink or basin,
cover the overflow hole with a damp cloth to build up the pressure while you are using a plunger.

For bad bathroom stains
mix a paste of peroxide and cream of tartar. Scrub with a small brush and rinse thoroughly. If stains persist, reapply the paste and add a drop or two of household ammonia. Let stand for two hours and scrub again.

Before you start to clean tiles,
run the shower at its hottest water setting. The steam will help loosen the dirt and make for easier cleaning.

Lemon oil keeps tiles shinier longer
and helps keep water stains from building up.

For gleaming chrome taps or fixtures,
try rubbing alcohol.

To create a fresh, clean aroma in the bathroom,
toss a sheet of fabric conditioner in the wastebasket.

Or dab a bit of your favourite perfume on a light bulb.
It floods the room with scent when the light is turned on.

Save those soap slivers!
Mix them in the blender with some water and make your own liquid soap.

Or
collect them in an old nylon stocking and hang near an outside tap for a fast outdoor clean-ups.

To remove hairspray from your bathroom mirror
use rubbing alcohol.

Kerosene will remove scum and spots from bathroom fixtures.

Make your own ceramic-tile cleaner

by mixing quarter of a cup of baking soda, half a cup of white vinegar, one cup of household ammonia and 1 gallon/ 4.5 litres of warm water in a bucket. Stir, and apply with a sponge or brush. This will not keep between cleaning, so you will need to make a fresh batch each time and always wear rubber gloves as the solution is quite harsh. But, the tiles will be 'mirror clean'!

Reduce steam in the bathroom

by running cold water into the bath before turning the hot water on. The less steam you get, the fewer mould spots.

Clean soap splashes from tiles

with a solution of one part white vinegar to four parts water. Rinse and wipe down.

If hard water has caused splashes

on tiles or glass that are hard to remove, rub neat malt vinegar over the surface. Leave for ten minutes before rinsing off.

Soap lasts longer

if stored in the airing cupboard for a few months. It also adds a lovely fragrance to the things you keep in there.

THE HOME

....

'Cleaning your house while your kids
   are growing
Is like shovelling the walk before it
   stops snowing.'
Phyllis Diller

Floors

....

'The white-washed wall, the nicely sanded floor.'
Oliver Goldsmith

For heel marks on hard floors,
> wipe with kerosene or turpentine or use a pencil eraser.

Nail-varnish spills can be left to solidify.
> When just barely pliable, peel off.

Be careful when cleaning quarry or ceramic tiles.
> Although the tiles are very tough the grout surrounding them will not be. Rinse thoroughly to prevent the grout deteriorating.

Dark-coloured floors show up scuffs, dust and scratch marks
> whilst black heel marks show up more easily on light-coloured floors. Consider your options or face a lifetime on your knees scrubbing!

When choosing a mop consider this:
cotton mops need breaking in, but will dry a floor faster than the alternatives. Rayon mops require no break-in and will immediately absorb water, often absorbing seven times the mops weight. Blended mops can offer the best of both worlds: no break-in time, plus immediate absorbency!

To eliminate the redepositing of soil as you mop,
frequently flip the mop-head as you work.

Top mop tips:
always use cold water, not hot. Keep your back straight. Do not twist your spine. Bend at the knees, not your back. Use your arm muscles to move the mop in a figure-of-eight pattern. (It's all good exercise too!)

Wipe your guests' feet for them!
Most visitors don't wipe their feet. Their minds are focused on where they are

going, or they are keeping pace with the people behind them. Ensure you have a good length of matting on arrival.

A good hallway mat should be four lazy steps in length

(15 ft/4.5 m). By the time the average visitor has taken those steps, most of the grit and dirt is off their shoes and onto the mat where you can collect it regularly.

Brooms can be cleaned

with a mild detergent and warm water.

Storing your broom on its head

will damage the bristles. Nail a couple of cotton reels into a cupboard door or wall to hang the head on, with the handle hanging down, to preserve the life of your broom.

Check that your broom handle is the right length for you to avoid back strain.

Held upright, it should reach the bridge of your nose.

Use a mop for one job only
– mark the handle or use a different
colour mop to indicate its purpose.

For a clean, sweet smelling sponge,
just run it through a full cycle in the top
rack of your dish-washer.

For really mucky floors,
a squeegee is perfect for scraping up the
mud and grime before you give it a wash.

When you are applying polish,
wrap an old towel around a broom head
to buff it up afterwards. The towel will
ensure there isn't excess polish left
on the wood and will also bring up a
wonderful shine.

Or, bring up a shine
by rubbing the floor with a bundle of old
nylon tights.

Linoleum and vinyl

are often used in children's rooms in place of carpets. If little fingers mark it with wax crayons, there's no need for tears, a little bit of silver polish will remove the damage.

Also, remove grease marks

from vinyl by holding an ice cube on to the stain before washing it with some soapy water.

Slate floors

will come up a treat if a little milk is added to the final rinse.

Scratched floors look messy

but the scratches are often caused by old mops. Change the sponge on your mop before it gets too worn down and make sure your floor stays looking as good as new.

To clean a dirty mat,

put it in a bin bag and shake it around.
The dust will stay in the bag rather than
settling on the rest of your furniture.

Keep dust from flying around

– empty the contents of your vacuum
onto a damp newspaper.

If you've dropped a glass,

use a piece of white bread to 'blot' up the
tiny slivers of glass. Make sure you've
cleared all the shards up.

To clean a wooden floor,

scatter damp tea leaves over it to hold on
to the dust when sweeping.

**Make your old linoleum floor look as good as
new.**

Wipe it down with one part fresh milk
mixed with one part turpentine. Rub into
the floor and polish with a warm soft
cloth.

Get your quarry floor shining

– use live natural yoghurt to wash it
down.

Remove shoe marks from linoleum

by scrubbing gently with fine steel wool
dipped in white spirit or turpentine.

To clean a varnished floor,

try adding instant tea granules to your
bucket of soapy water.

For scratched woodwork,

you can minimize the damage by dabbing
with cotton wool that's been dipped in
diluted tea.

Scratches on dark woods

can be disguised by rubbing with the cut
edge of a Brazil nut.

For light woods,

use a wax crayon or shoe polish in a
colour that blends in.

Technical Equipment

'I want to clean television up.'
Mary Whitehouse (attributed)

To clean your TV/video remote control unit,
first take the batteries out. Then with
a paint brush and a bit of methylated
spirits, give it a good scrub. Leave for half
an hour and it will be as good as new.

Dusting your TV?
Eliminate static electricity from your
screen by wiping with a used sheet of
fabric conditioner. It will help prevent
dust resettling.

To clean between computer keys,
use cotton buds.

Clean the ball of a computer mouse
with a cotton bud dampened with
alcohol.

To clean ink and ribbon fibre from typewriter keys,

roll Silly Putty into a ball and very carefully press into the keys.

Soft Furnishings

'You should have a softer pillow than my heart.'
Lord Byron

Wash your feather pillows while imagining you're in the vineyards of France.

Dissolve a handful of soap flakes in a bath of warm water. Place pillows in and tread with bare feet to remove the dirt. Repeat and rinse, spin in the washing machine and hang up to dry.

Tired-looking pillows can be brought back to life

by making an opening in the seam and pumping air in with a bicycle pump. Remember to stitch the seam back up!

Stick curtain hooks into a bar of soap
and you'll be able to attach them to your
fabric with a lot less hassle.

Candle wax on your tablecloth?
Place a blotter or brown paper bag over
the spot and put a hot iron on top. After
a few minutes, the wax will be absorbed
by the blotter and the cloth will look as
good as new.

**Alternatively, if you get candle wax on your
tablecloth,**
heat a spoon over the candle. Then place
a piece of wet newspaper over the wax
and rub the hot spoon over the newspaper
to melt the wax, which will then come
off the tablecloth and stick to the paper.

For an instant food and drink spot remover
use shaving cream. Apply, blot into the
stain, wash with water and blot dry.

Delicate tapestries or needlepoint coverings
can be safely cleaned with a baby's soft
hairbrush.

Once dirty, it's impossible to get net curtains really clean,
> so wash them regularly.

Make invisible repairs in your net curtains
> – dab colourless nail varnish on the torn edges and hold them together until the varnish is dry.

Blast the dust off a pleated lamp shade
> with a hair-dryer.

Or,
> use an old toothbrush.

Wash fabric lampshades in warm water,
> then dry them with a hair-dryer on cool. This tightens up the material so that the shade looks like new.

Make soft furnishings last longer
> – simply spray them with Scotchguard or any waterproofing spray that you would use on suede shoes.

Leather sofas

should be buffed up with a mixture of linseed oil and vinegar. Simply heat through equal amounts of each, then allow to cool to room temperature and apply with a clean duster. Your sofa will gleam!

For a toddler's room,

try shower curtains instead of fabric drapes. However grubby the little fingers that tug at them, they will always wipe clean and they come in lots of fun designs.

The armrests of a chair quickly get mucky,

so clean them up by rubbing with a loaf of bread.

Don't ruin beautiful chintz.

Always iron the wrong side to protect the special glaze.

Clean velour upholstery

with a solution of warm water and washing-up liquid. Dip some muslin into the mixture and wipe over the fabric.

Remove the stamens from lilies
to prevent the pollen from staining
clothes and furnishing fabrics. Wipe up
any pollen that falls on to polished wood
surfaces because, if left, it will eat into
the wood.

If you do get stamen dust onto some fabric,
lift it off by dabbing with some sticky
tape – don't rub it as you will simply
spread the dust and you'll never get rid
of it.

Vacuum your curtains
every few weeks and you won't need to
have them dry-cleaned so often.

**To avoid taking down curtains when washing
windows,**
drape them through a coat hanger and
hang them from the curtain rod.

To get rid of dog or cat hair on sofas or rugs,
blot the fabric with a damp rubber glove.

Alternatively,
> to collect cat or dog hairs from furniture
> use a sheet of fabric conditioner.

Walls and Ceilings

....

'Either that wallpaper goes or I do.'
Oscar Wilde's last words

When washing walls,
> start off at the bottom and work upwards
> so that any dirty trickles are absorbed
> by the already wet surface. (Everybody,
> seemingly logically, starts at the top and
> works down!) Skirting boards are usually
> the dirtiest part of the room, so leave
> them till last.

Gloss-painted walls
> can be washed, but always give a final
> wipe with a towel to avoid streaky marks
> appearing when they dry.

To clean wallpaper,
use stale but still slightly moist bread. This gets the marks off without the need for soap and water.

To clean rough plaster walls,
bunch old nylon stockings together into a ball and rub against the wall. Unlike most cloths, the stockings won't leave any little pieces of fabric behind.

For crayon marks try using silver polish.

Or scrub the marks with some toothpaste
and wipe off with a damp cloth.

If that doesn't work, to remove crayon marks,
apply a thin coat of rubber-cement glue and allow to dry thoroughly, then 'roll' it off. If a colour stain remains, try rubbing a little liquid detergent mixed with a few drops of household ammonia.

To remove remnants of Blu tac from walls,
roll a ball of Blu tac over the spot and what's left will come off.

To blow dust or cobwebs out of corners,
use a balloon pump or a bicycle pump.

Small irritating marks on a ceiling
can be blotted out with a little white
shoe polish.

If a ceiling gets really grubby
or smoke stained, it is often quicker
to whitewash it than clean it. A pair
of swimming goggles is a good idea to
protect your eyes when painting.

To whitewash a ceiling,
it is easier to use a new sponge mop than
to perch on a ladder with a roller.

Don't try to clean unpainted bricks
– water will make any marks worse.

Leave natural walls
to acquire an attractively aged
appearance.

Tiling all the wall space

in a bathroom can look stunning but be a
pain to keep looking gleaming. A squeegee
will do the trick in no time.

Grubby marks on embossed wallpaper

can be a problem. A clean, soft-bristled
toothbrush will help to remove them.

Mouldings and cornicing

can be awkward to clean thoroughly. Put
some detergent into a garden spray bottle
to get into all the nooks and crannies.
After wiping, spray again with clean water
to make sure no detergent is left lingering.

A terry nappy is good for wiping cornicing

because the loops get into all the detail.

Dirty marks round light switches

can be removed using a soft india-rubber.

To clean light switches

whilst protecting expensive surrounding
wallpaper, make a cardboard template.

Carpets

....

'Snug as a bug in a rug.'
Benjamin Franklin

When using a damp cloth to sponge out a stain,

re-wet and wring out the cloth between each go – otherwise you're just sponging in the stain with a dirty cloth.

Move furniture with ease –

put foil pie dishes under each leg and the furniture can be slid easily over the carpet.

To neutralize odours and discourage pests,

liberally sprinkle bicarbonate of soda on your carpets and leave for 15 minutes before vacuuming up.

Raise dents in carpets

made by heavy furniture by rubbing with the edge of a coin.

Alternatively,
remove dents in carpet pile by covering
with a damp cloth and then quickly
placing a hot iron on top. The steam lifts
the pile.

**Another trick for removing furniture dents in
carpets:**
squirt the area with water and fluff with
a fork.

To raise flattened carpet pile
over larger areas, use a really hot steam
iron. Hold the iron over the area without
allowing it to touch the carpet. Brush the
pile briskly back and forth with the other
hand.

To clean up muddy paw marks or footprints,
resist the temptation to do something
about them straightaway. Leave the mud
to dry completely before vacuuming it
up. Sponge off any marks that are left
with carpet shampoo.

To vacuum the fringes on rugs,
> slip an old stocking over the end of the hose attachment.

This is also useful if someone drops a contact lens on the floor.
> The stocking will stop the lens from disappearing into the bowels of the vacuum cleaner.

Grubby lambskin rugs can be brushed with lots of dry powdered magnesia.
> Leave for a day, shake well and brush thoroughly.

The average small doormat
> is fairly useless for trapping dirt. Fit the first few feet of your hall with coconut matting instead of carpet to really capture dust and mud. Edge it with some simple brass tread and it will look stylish too.

Always vacuum your carpet as you would mow your lawn,
> in neat rows, back and forth, so that you don't miss a spot. Each section needs at least two or three passes.

Sooty footprints:
sprinkle with salt, let stand for
30 minutes, then vacuum. On light-
coloured carpets, try an art gum eraser.

Vacuum your carpets regularly.
Oily dirt, especially, attracts more oily
dirt and frequent vacuuming will reduce
the build up.

Do not over wet carpets when using detergents.
The detergents are chemically active
enough and over-wetting can cause
brown-out, carpet shrinkage, adhesion
problems and other nightmares!

Never apply carpet protector to a dirty carpet,
you will seal in the dirt. Shampoo the
carpet to get it completely clean and then
apply.

Vacuuming is hard work
at the best of times. Change your
vacuum bag before it gets too full –
a full bag is less efficient and makes
the task twice as difficult.

If your vacuum cleaner's hose gets clogged with dust,

you can knock out the clog with a broom handle pushed carefully through the length.

Brush the dust from the corners and edges of carpets

with a hand brush and then vacuum it up.

If the pollen from flowers has got onto your carpet or fabric,

lift it off gently with sticky tape so that you don't rub it in and leave an indelible stain.

Freshen carpets

by sprinkling liberally with salt, oatmeal or cornflour. Leave for a couple of hours and then vacuum.

Revive the colour in a faded carpet

using a mix of one part vinegar to two parts boiling water. Soak a cloth in this solution, rub into the carpet and watch the colours come back.

Fountain pen ink should be blotted up
   with kitchen paper towels and sponged
   with cold water until the stain lifts.
   Use carpet shampoo to finish off.

Pet puddles needn't be a problem.
   To get rid of stains from a carpet, mix
   equal parts of white vinegar and cool
   water, blot up, rinse and allow to dry.

To clean scorch marks,
   use the edge of a coin to loosen the burn
   fibres and then sweep them up.

Really bad scorch marks
   are impossible to get rid of, but you can
   minimize the effect by trimming with
   a pair of scissors.

To make sure a carpet stays 'up' after a wet clean,
   vacuum immediately after cleaning,
   don't walk on it and leave it to dry
   overnight.

To clean up big spillages,
> use a cloth dampened with lukewarm
> water to sponge the stain immediately –
> it's better than leaving it to dry and then
> using a chemical cleaner.

Windows and Curtains

'C-l-e-a-n, clean, verb active, to make
  bright, to scour.
W-i-n, win, d-e-r, winder, a casement. When
  the boy knows this out of the book, he
  goes and does it.'
Charles Dickens, Nicholas Nickleby

Ugly insect or fly-spots on windows
> can be removed with cold tea.

**Never clean windows on a very cold or frosty
day**
> – the glass will be brittle and liable to
> break.

However, don't clean them on a really sunny day either

– the glass will dry too quickly, leaving smears.

So ... ideally, wash windows on a dull day!

Dull, cool weather is ideal for window cleaning, especially if there is a little damp in the air to show up all the marks.

Windows can be made to sparkle

using a little vinegar and water mixed together (methylated spirits works just as well). Work the mixture round the glass with a little chamois leather.

Alternatively,

to make windows and mirrors sparkle use scrunched-up paper coffee filters.

Windows can be buffed using crumpled newspaper;

the printer's ink gives added sparkle.

Clean windows

with a solution of half a cup of household ammonia, the same of white vinegar and two tablespoons of corn starch in a bucket of warm water.

When you've cleaned your windows,

for a really fine shine, after the windows are dry, rub a clean blackboard eraser over them.

To clean windowsills,

pour a little diluted rubbing alcohol on a cloth and rub the entire surface. The spots will disappear and the sills will look freshly painted.

When cleaning windows,

make your strokes vertical on the inside and horizontal on the outside so that you know where any remaining smears are coming from.

Here's a pithy tip ... for sparkling glass.

If your lemons are over-ripe, squeeze them into hot water and use them to clean your windows.

To reduce the need for artificial lights,
make sure you clean the windows
thoroughly because dirty windows
can reduce the natural light by around
20 per cent.

Clean aluminium window frames with cream silver polish.

To keep the corners of windowpanes free of dust and moisture,
save the ends of white candles and rub
the wax on the corners of the wood.

Louvered windows and doors are easy to clean
with a 2-in/5-cm wide paint brush dipped
in a mild soap solution. Lightly towel
dry. Or dab lighter fluid on a cloth and
rub gently.

Cure condensation
by cleaning the affected area with bleach,
then dry out with lots of warmth and
ventilation.

Venetian blinds can get filthy
but take hours to clean. Pop on a pair of
damp cotton gardening gloves and run
your fingers along each slat.

For gleaming Venetian or mini blinds,
saturate a cloth with rubbing alcohol and
wrap around a rubber spatula to clean
both a bottom and a top slat at the same
time.

If they are really filthy, soak blinds in the bath.
While wearing a pair of cotton gardening
gloves, wipe each slat clean. Then hang
the blinds over the bath to dry.

Dull net curtains can be transformed
back into gleaming white by putting a
denture-cleaning tablet into water and
soaking the curtains.

Furniture polish on a curtain rail
will make curtains run smoothly.

General Cleaning

'Housekeeping ain't no joke.'
Louisa May Alcott

Hygiene is vital. Colour-code your cleaning cloths and sponges
– use a green one for the toilet, a blue one for the sink, a yellow one for the cooker, etc...

When the artificial coal in an electric fire becomes faded and grey,
soak a cloth in blackcurrant jelly and rub over the coals. Leave to dry and they'll come up really glossy.

To clean in the tiniest nooks and crannies,
use a camera lens-cleaning brush, the sort with an air-sac attached.

To get rid of grease,
blot with a kitchen paper towel and sprinkle corn starch on the stain. Rub off the corn starch when it has soaked up all the grease.

For difficult areas

such as stair railings, chairs etc. use old socks as mitts to clean. (Just make sure they're clean before you start!)

Dust louvered doors by wrapping a cloth around a ruler.

Spray the cloth with polish and run the flat end across each slat.

To remove sticky-back shelf lining,

use your hair-dryer to 'warm' the adhesive. Use the lowest setting first, holding the dryer over a small area. When it is warmed enough, it should just lift away from the shelf. Continue warming and lifting small sections until the job is done.

To clean a room quickly of cigarette smoke odour,

soak a towel in equal parts of hot water and vinegar, wring it out completely and wave it like a flag over your head several

times as you move around the room.
(You will feel very silly but your room
will smell wonderful!)

**Also, if smoky smells are a problem, sprinkle
baking soda**

into the carpet, leave for 30 minutes,
then vacuum.

To get rid of cigar fumes,

leave a bowl of cider vinegar in the room
overnight.

When cleaning mirrors and glassware,

light and shadows will play tricks on
your eyes! After you've cleaned the
glassware, kneel down and look up for
streaks.

To make tidying less of a chore,

don't save it all up for the weekend,
choose one room to have a go at each day
of the week. Come the weekend you'll
only have time for fun …

For those difficult-to-get-at corners

and around the base of taps, save your old toothbrushes; they are ideal for awkward cleaning jobs.

Make life easier when cleaning.

Put some detergent on, say, a floor or a sink then move on to the next job leaving it to work for a while. By the time you return the detergent will have really got into the dirt and your task will be half done for you.

Car wax makes an ideal cleanser

and polish for ceramics. Apply it generously and give it a wipe with a soft duster before it is completely dry. Not only will it clean your tiles a treat, but its natural waterproofing will keep them looking good for longer.

Sticky label marks

can be stubborn to remove from glass. Try rubbing the marks with a little peanut butter on a piece of some soft cotton wool.

Most people just spread dust about when dusting.
Make sure you don't by regularly shaking the duster outside between jobs.

Mildew can ruin books.
Sprinkle the book with talcum powder, leave for a few days then brush off with a soft brush or cloth.

Remove a greasy mark from paper
or a book by placing some blotting paper either side of the sheet and ironing on a low heat.

To remove cellulose-based adhesives
and model aircraft glue use non-oily nail-varnish remover or acetone.

Don't leave cleaning products under the kitchen sink
where children can get at them.

Clutter
makes a room much harder to clean. As a rule, if you haven't used something

for six months you probably won't use it again – why not let a charity shop benefit and cut your housework down at the same time.

Dirty dishcloths cause germs.

Always dry yours out thoroughly before storing away – bacteria love nothing more than a nice, warm damp bed ...

Dustpans and brushes

are always overlooked but they get filthy – wash yours out thoroughly at least once a month. They will be much more effective at picking up dirt and more hygienic too.

Soaking slimy sponges or cloths in vinegar

will freshen them up and extend their use.

Dusting can be done in half the time

if you use a duster in each hand.

Create a super-efficient duster
by soaking it, when new, in a mix of
equal parts of paraffin, vinegar and water
... it will literally lift up dirt rather than
scatter dust around a room.

Beds should be aired daily,
not just made as soon as you get up. We
actually lose up to half a pint of moisture
every night, so throw back the covers
each morning and let your bed breathe.

Another good reason for airing your bed ...
little pests and bed mites love nothing
more than a lovely, cosy made up bed.
Leave your covers back and they'll soon
move house.

If you are suddenly surprised by visitors
and the house is a mess ... don't panic,
just plump up the scatter cushions
and spray a quick blast of furniture
polish into the air to create a good first
impression!

No time to clean but you want to give the impression that you've been busy?

Spray furniture polish behind the radiators. The heat will disperse the scent round the room.

Never clean a light bulb that is switched on

or has only just been turned off.

Clean light bulbs regularly with a cloth moistened with methylated spirirts.

When cleaning light bulbs,

rub a little vanilla essence around the bulb with a soft cloth. When the light is switched back on, a lovely smell will be gently released.

If a bulb breaks

while you are removing it, press an old cork onto the broken glass and twist to remove the rest of the light bulb.

Clean your radiators

as well as the furniture. Dust can insulate radiators, keeping down the amount of heat that they give off.

But cleaning *behind* radiators

is tricky and often gets overlooked
altogether. A sock placed over a broom
handle will reach the parts other cleaners
cannot reach!

To keep decorative feathers clean,

sprinkle with talcum powder and then
use a hair-dryer to blow the powder off.

Clean a circular fan

with an old sock over your hand.

Line the top of a tall bookcase with old newspaper.

When you want to remove the dust, just
throw away the paper and replace it. This
works for the tops of kitchen cabinets as
well.

Alternatively,

use a new paint brush to brush off the
dust.

Make your own polishing pad

by cutting up some old tights and putting them in a cotton bag. A little one is ideal for polishing, a bigger one brilliant for preventing household knee … two tips in one!

Save wear and tear on your rubber gloves

– put sticking plasters on the inside of each finger of the gloves.

Make sure dirt stays in the dustpan

– spray the inside of the pan with furniture polish so that the dust has something to stick to.

Cork table mats can be washed

by putting them in a bowl of clean water and rubbing each with a pumice stone. Rinse under cold water and dry in a cool place.

Tapestry work can be sprinkled with powdered magnesia.

Work in well with your fingertips wrapped in a clean cloth. Leave for several hours at least, then brush out gently.

To clean the inside of a clock,

soak a small piece of cotton wool in kerosene or paraffin and place in the base of the clock. Leave for a few days. This will draw down all the dust and leave the clock clean.

Keep pewter clean

by rubbing it with a cabbage leaf. Finish off by polishing it with a soft cloth.

Alternatively,

rub the pewter with petrol and leave to dry. When it's dry, rub over with hot beer. Leave this to dry as well and then buff with a soft cloth.

To clean engraved pewter,

mix wood ash with some water into a paste. Rub this over the pewter and then polish off.

Bring up the shine on silver

by rubbing it with a piece of rhubarb.

Damp dusters

pick up dust more effectively.

Pin a plastic bag to your clothes

as you work your way round the house. You can drop in little bits of rubbish as you go without constantly running up and down stairs.

Blow dust off dried or artificial flowers

using a hair-dryer (on its lowest setting).

To clean silk flowers

– put them in a large paper bag with a generous scoop of salt. Shake vigorously until all the dust is removed from the flowers.

Changing duvet covers needn't end up as a wrestling match.

Put one corner of the duvet into its cover and hold it in position with a clothes peg. Repeat with the other corner and shake the duvet down into the cover.

Clean scissors and needles
with surgical spirit; it's a great way to remove fabric glue.

For home-made furniture polish,
mix one part lemon juice with two parts olive oil.

Don't throw away empty washing powder boxes.
Use them to keep magazines or files in. Just cut a large corner away and cover the box with left-over wallpaper or wrapping paper.

If you've mislaid your dustpan,
wet the edge of a newspaper, brush the dirt over the edge and roll up the paper.

Clean brass handles
with lemon juice.

Preserve the shine on a slate hearth
by spraying with WD40.

Stop cast iron from rusting
by wiping with olive oil or sunflower oil.

To get rid of the craze on ceramic ware,
soak the piece in baby disinfectant.

Save money
– cut your steel-wool pads in half so they
go twice as far.

Preserve steel-wool pads for longer
by keeping them in soapy water. This
will stop them from rusting.

But, if your steel-wool scourers are rusting
wrap them in kitchen foil after use.

Clean vases regularly
with bleach – not washing-up liquid –
to kill the bacteria residue. Flowers are
dirty things!

To brighten cut-glass jugs or vases,
fill them with wet potato peelings and
leave to stand for a day. Remove and
rinse well.

Don't waste your money on expensive leaf shine,
give your potted plants a good wipe down with milk.

To remove the black yucky mould that can grow in damp corners,
use an old toothbrush, dipped in a mixture of water and bleach.

Leave your wastebaskets smelling sweet
– put a sheet of fabric conditioner in the bottom.

Solve the problem of unwanted blobs of chewing gum
by placing a bag of ice cubes over the gum to freeze it. Tap the frozen gum with a hammer to break it up and then pick off as much as you can. Any remaining bits can be removed using a cloth dipped in methylated spirits.

Dirty ashtrays look so ugly.
Keep them clean with an old shaving brush.

Some fluffy toys can't be washed.
When teddy needs a clean, shake him in a plastic bag with some bicarbonate of soda then brush him well afterwards. (And there'll be no tearful nights waiting for him to dry either!)

Bronze is improved
by regularly cleaning the surface with dark brown shoe polish and buffing vigorously with a soft cloth.

To get rid of sticky label adhesive
wipe the surface with methylated spirits.

Alternatively,
sprinkle talcum powder on to the adhesive and rub with your finger to remove.

Fountain pens
are fiddly things to clean, so they're best soaked in some neat vinegar for ten or so minutes then left to dry on some blotting paper.

To shift wax from metal candlesticks,
carefully pour boiling water over the
candlestick; this will melt the wax.

Alternatively,
to remove wax from a candlestick, use a
hair-dryer on a low setting to blow hot
air over the surface until the wax has
melted.

Keep night-light candles burning for ages.
Put a pinch of salt in each one.

To stop candles dripping,
sharpen the ends like a pencil. This stops
the wax from collecting in a pool and
then suddenly spilling over.

Candles burn more evenly
and won't drip if you pop them in a
freezer before use.

Strong cooking smells will be minimized
by lighting a candle in the kitchen while
you're cooking. (This is also a useful tip
for the loo!)

Spray candles with your favourite perfume.
As they burn down, they release the smell into the room. Ideal for candle-lit dinners!

Sticking doors can be unstuck
by rubbing the sticky edge with a candle.

If your furniture drawers keep sticking,
try rubbing vegetable soap on the runners.

To make your own fragrant drawer liners,
simply cut out left-over wallpaper and spray with your favourite perfume.

Or, try using a scented tumble-drier sheet instead.

When cleaning away ashes from a fireplace,
sprinkle damp tea leaves over them to keep the dust down.

Remove soot from bricks

around a fireplace by scrubbing with neat malt vinegar. Rinse well and then blot the surface with a sponge.

Furniture

....

'I make no secret of the fact that I would rather lie on a sofa than sweep beneath it. But you have to be efficient if you're going to be lazy.'
Shirley Conran

Remove water marks

by mixing a paste of butter and cigarette ash. Apply the paste to a damp cloth, buff then polish.

If you don't have any cigarette ash,

try rubbing the mark with some mayonnaise on a soft cloth.

Or try toothpaste

applied to the water mark with a damp cloth.

Children's stickers

can be removed from wood by 'painting' the sticker with white vinegar, letting it soak in and then scraping off.

If you are worried about your table,

put some cling film across the wood before laying the table. If you are concerned about hot dishes burning the wood, put a blanket underneath the tablecloth.

Really dusty wicker furniture

can take hours to clean. Try giving it a blast with a hair-dryer first to get rid of the worst.

Or,

a soft toothbrush is ideal for getting into all the grooves on wicker.

Likewise, try using a toothbrush on carved wood

– it is particularly good for getting polish out of any crevices.

Scratches on wood

can be concealed by rubbing in a little cod liver oil.

To get rid of rings or minor scratches on wood,

cover with petroleum jelly and leave for 24 hours. Rub it into the wood, wipe off the excess and then polish as normal.

Polish wood

with metal polish instead of the normal woody kind and it should come up a treat.

Saggy cane seats can be re-tightened

by wetting the top and bottom of the seat with hot, soapy water. Leave the chair to dry in the open air. As the cane dries, it shrinks and tightens up. Unfortunately, this method doesn't work on saggy bottoms!

If you've lost a castor off the bottom of a chair,

place a cotton reel there instead. If it shows, colour it first with dark felt-tip pen.

White rings on waxed surfaces

can be removed using a paste made from salt and olive oil. Leave the stain covered with the paste overnight and then wipe off. The surface can then be rewaxed.

Remove greasy marks from wood veneers

by sprinkling the surface with talcum powder. Cover with a couple of sheets of tissue paper and, using the tip of a warm iron, gently press onto the surface to draw out the grease.

You can raise dents in wood

by placing a damp cloth over the dent and holding a warm iron (don't get it too hot) over the cloth for a few minutes. The moisture from the cloth swells the grain. Allow the wood to dry before polishing.

Alternatively,

repair a dent in wood by filling with a few drops of clear nail varnish.

Instruments

....

'Music washes away from the soul the dust of everyday life.'
Red Auerbach

To clean ivory piano keys,
squeeze a little fluoride toothpaste onto a damp cloth. Rub the keys quite hard and buff with a soft dry cloth.

Alternatively,
you can try the Victorian way and clean the keys with milk.

To polish your piano keys properly,
never spray directly onto the keys. Spray onto a cloth and work from the top of the key to the bottom. Don't polish sideways.

To help your music sheets last just that bit longer,
laminate them and store them in a flat box.

To clean the inside of your guitar
– fill it with uncooked rice, give it a really good shake and then empty.

You can clean your brass instrument
cheaply and effectively with warm soapy water.

Get the most out of your wind instrument
by cleaning it as soon as you have finished with it.

Clean your clarinet properly
by attaching a piece of flannelette sheet to a knitting needle and shoving that down your instrument.

Painters and Decorators

'You are looking as fresh as paint.'
Francis Smedley

Sometimes, when a house gets really grubby,
for instance if it has been empty for
some time, it can be cheaper and more
effective simply to redecorate. But
decorating itself is a messy business,
so take note ...

If your paint brushes have hardened,
soften them by dipping in a pan of
boiling vinegar for a few minutes.

**Don't waste turpentine by throwing it out
each time.**
Pour any unused liquid into a screw-top
bottle. After a few days the sediment
will settle leaving you with lots of clean
turpentine at the top.

Never stand brushes in water when you take a break

> – it can swell the wooden handle and rust the metal ferrule.

To soak a brush without leaving it in the bottom of a jar,

> drill a hole half way down the handle and push a pencil through to balance the brush across the opening of a jar.

To clean brushes,

> put the paint cleaner in a plastic bag along with the paint brush. You can then rub the bristles with your fingers to get all the paint out.

Don't spend hours washing out rollers each night,

> just rinse out and place in a plastic bag and they will be ready to go in the morning.

When you have finished with your paste brush,

> rinse it in salted water before washing because this gets rid of the paste easily and leaves the brush nice and soft.

Always keep white spirit in a jam jar with a lid
to stop any evaporation.

Wear surgical gloves
to keep your hands clean when painting.

To clean an artist's palette
use a mixture of white spirit and soap.

After a Fire

Nothing causes more dirt and damage than a fire. If you're unfortunate enough to have needed the fire service to hose down your house, here are a few tips to get things back to normal.

If you must use your mattress temporarily,
sun dry the mattress on both sides and cover with plastic sheeting. However, mattresses will need replacing – as will pillows: it is almost impossible to get the smell out of them, as feathers and foam retain odour.

Let rugs and carpets dry out thoroughly.

Clean with a wet/dry vacuum or water-extractor carpet-cleaning machine. They will remove the standing water and dirt. Rinse by using vinegar and water in the tank of the machine. Dry the rugs as quickly as possible. A fan turned on the rug will speed the drying. Any moisture remaining at the base will quickly rot the rug, causing it to fall apart.

Most dishes

can be soaked in one tablespoon bleach to 1 gallon/4.5 litres of lukewarm water for 30 minutes prior to washing. Wash in hot soapy water. Dishwashers are excellent for this purpose.

When water is underneath lino

it can cause odour, and rot or warp a wood floor, which could become a major expense. If this happens, remove the entire sheet of lino. If glued, a heat lamp will soften it so you can roll it up without breaking it.

Walls may be washed down while still wet.
Use a mild soap solution and wear rubber gloves. Work from the floor up, a small area at a time. Rinse with clear water. Work quickly when washing wallpaper so that the paper does not become soaked. Wash ceilings last. *Do not paint until dry.*

Dry, heat and ventilate rooms
for several days to dry plaster and paper. If mildewed, wipe with a cloth wrung with soap. Repaste edges or loosened sections of paper.

VALUABLES

....

'Gold is for the mistress,
Silver for the maid,
Copper for the craftsman,
Cunning is his trade...'
Rudyard Kipling

Silver

···

If you don't want to spend too long being the 'maid' ...

To polish silver effectively
use your bare fingers. You'll find they work much better at getting rid of tarnish than any polish.

Remove wax easily from silver candlesticks
by placing them in the fridge overnight. It's then easy to pick off.

To keep silver clean
rub on a mixture of lemon and salt, then dry with a soft cloth.

To stop silver jewellery from tarnishing,
wrap it in black tissue paper.

Alternatively,
wrap it in cling film so it doesn't tarnish.

If you are packing silver away for any length of time,

wrap it in a clean T-shirt and store away from the light.

Look after the family silver

– never put silver or plate cutlery next to stainless steel in the dishwasher.

You can clean your silver jewellery

with minty toothpaste. Rinse thoroughly in warm water afterwards.

To clean engraved or embossed silver,

apply the polish with a small toothbrush which will get into all the lines and curves.

Alternatively,

a cotton wool bud will do the trick

Gold

....

'All that glisters is not gold,
Often have you heard that told.'
William Shakespeare

Gold chains

need careful handling. Soapy water is
the best thing to clean them with, but
try rubbing the gold gently in a chamois
leather afterwards to really make them
sparkle.

When washing up,

attach your precious rings to a safety pin
and pin them to your clothing.

To prevent your gold rings from getting misshapen,

dented or scratched – cover your car
steering wheel with some soft foam or
fabric. (Apparently gripping the wheel
too tight is the most common cause of
damage.)

Don't be conned into buying expensive gold cleaners,
most are just variations on common household bleach.

The best solution for cleaning gold
is warm water, mild detergent and a small splash of ammonia.

For really sparkling gold
soak it for several minutes in gin!

The best way to bring up a nine-carat shine
is with a soft-bristled toothbrush.

And, the best thing to buff up gold jewellery
is a spectacle cleaning cloth.

To store your gold
and silver without damage, line your jewellery box with an empty egg tray, so you can keep each piece of jewellery in a separate compartment.

To stop jewellery becoming tarnished,
place a piece of chalk in your trinket box.

To maintain a gleam,
remove all gold before bathing. The
soapy water simply builds up a film and
your precious jewellery will soon look
dull.

**Make sure you don't lose your valuables
while you're in the bath or shower.**
Hang a few hooks inside your bathroom
cabinet. Not only will your jewellery
be safely away from plug holes, but also
away from the damaging steam.

Gems and Stones

'Goodness what beautiful diamonds.'
'Goodness had nothing to do with it!'
Mae West

A good general cleaner
is a weak solution of washing-up liquid
in warm water with a little drop of
ammonia.

Useful cleaning tools

can be old toothbrushes or mascara wands.

Emeralds

are naturally fragile – always get them cleaned professionally.

Never put your emeralds

in hot water – the gems will absorb the liquid and crack.

Opals are very porous,

so avoid washing them altogether. Instead, buff up with a soft chamois leather.

Wash real pearls

in very salty water. Let them dry and then polish with a piece of velvet.

The best way to keep pearls

clean is to wear them. Real pearls worn regularly absorb the moisture from your body to keep them looking lustrous.

Pearls should be the first thing that go on in the morning
and the last thing to come off at night.

Shine pearls with a dab of olive oil
and wipe dry with a chamois.

Clean artificial pearls
with a chamois leather. Just rub it carefully over the beads.

Clean amber
in some warm milk, dry and polish with a cloth of soft silk.

Jet can be cleaned
with soft breadcrumbs.

Cameos should never be immersed in water.
Use a brush dipped in the general cleaner (see page 107) to gently clean the surface. Rinse in the same way with clean water. Blot off the excess water and rub with a chamois leather.

You can wash jade from time to time
in soapy warm water.

Also, jade
should be handled as much as possible.

If your diamonds have lost their sparkle,
drop them into a glass of water, add one denture-cleaning tablet and leave for a couple of minutes.

Bring a shine to tortoiseshell
by rubbing it with almond oil.

To remove marks from tortoiseshell,
rub talcum powder over the mark with a cotton rag.

To protect ivory,
polish with a little almond oil and a soft cloth.

Ivory should never be washed

because it can discolour. Clean ivory only when absolutely necessary by using a cotton wool bud dampened in methylated spirits.

To clean coral,

lightly sponge with a weak detergent solution.

General

'Life is made up of marble and mud.'
Nathaniel Hawthorne

To clean delicate oil paintings

there's no need for fancy fluids. Gently rub the surface with a bit of spit on a cotton wool bud. Test a small area first (in case your spit is too corrosive!).

Surface dirt can be removed

from an oil or acrylic painting by rubbing with a bit of old bread.

When cleaning the glass of a painting,
> spray the cleaner onto your duster before polishing, not directly onto the glass. This stops the moisture from damaging the frame.

Clean gilt picture frames
> with a mixture made from one egg and a teaspoon of bicarbonate of soda.

Costume jewellery
> can still be expensive. Look after yours by cleaning it with a little baking powder then brushing off with a soft toothbrush.

Nothing is more invaluable than a treasured teddy. Keep yours looking pucker with carpet shampoo
> and then just fluff him up afterwards.

Next time you clean your watch,
> you can actually remove scratches on the face too. Just spend five or ten minutes gently rubbing the glass with metal polish, then wipe off with a soft duster.

Spectacles need regular cleaning,
but often go rather smeary. A little
eau-de-Cologne or some astringent face
toner wiped over the glass will prevent
the problem.

To clean antique luggage,
use saddle soap.

Give a stuffed animal a brilliant smile.
Wipe its teeth with a wet wipe to whiten
its fangs.

To clean dark fur,
dry some bran in the oven, rub it into the
fur and then cover with a warm blanket.
You should leave it like this for half an
hour before shaking the bran out and
then brushing the fur.

To clean light fur,
rub some cornflour into the fur and roll
it up in a warm blanket. Leave it like
this for 24 hours before shaking out and
brushing.

If you want to clean unpainted wax items,
wipe them down with softened butter.

If you want to impress coin collectors
don't polish a coin, use an old toothbrush
and scrub it with hot water.

To restore bead work
hand wash in lukewarm water and blow
dry gently with a hair-dryer.

Stop brass from tarnishing
by spraying it with furniture polish
and leaving it to dry. This covers the
brass with a thin layer of wax, which
protects it.

To clean the tops of old books,
gently rub with bread crumbs.

**Clean valuable old books that have vellum
bindings**
by dipping cotton wool in milk and
gently wiping over the covers. Finally,
clean off with a soft, dry cloth.

Laminated playing cards
can be effectively cleaned by rubbing
with some white bread.

Valuable embossed or gilded china
should be cleaned with a small eyebrow
brush kept specifically for the purpose.

Bone china should not be a museum piece.
Take it out and clean it every year.

To clean small glass ornaments,
put them in a sink and spray with liquid
window cleaner, rinse off, then dry them
on a towel.

When cleaning a chandelier,
you should always wear cotton gloves.
This stops you from leaving greasy finger
marks on the crystal. If you have to dry a
chandelier in situ, use a hair-dryer.

To clean delicate china figurines,
hold the base and work from top to
bottom. Brush off the dirt with a long-
haired, soft make-up brush dipped in a

warm solution of washing-up liquid (or soap flakes if the finish is matt). Rinse using the brush dipped in plain water and leave to dry on a paper towel.

To clean intricate porcelain

– place on a cloth in a plastic bowl. Put a solution of warm water and washing-up liquid in a spray bottle. Wash and then rinse the figure. Empty the water as it accumulates. Leave to dry on a towel.

STAINS

....

'Out damned spot.'
William Shakespeare

Carpets

....

*'They don't invite me to Balmoral
nowadays, which is a blessing; those
damned tartan carpets always put me off
my food.'*
George MacDonald Fraser

Catch a carpet stain within the first few days.

The longer a stain chemically reacts
with the carpet the harder it will be to
remove it.

Before shampooing or removing stains from carpet, test an old scrap.

Some carpets are extremely sensitive
to acid type cleaners and will lose their
colour quickly. Other carpets will be
sensitive to harsh alkalis.

To remove curry stains from carpets,

use a little lemon juice with water.

For bloodstains on the carpet,

sponge with cold water and blot firmly
with a towel as often as you need. Finish
off with carpet shampoo.

To remove a cigarette stain from the carpet,
pour a small amount of milk on the stain and leave it to soak in. This will dilute the colour and stop it browning. Then rub the stain with a raw potato and wash as normal.

Beer stains
can be removed from carpets with soda water.

Never overuse stain removers, detergents or shampoos
because the residue will stay in the carpet and prove impossible to remove.

Bathrooms

....

'Always go to the bathroom when you have a chance.'
King George V

For a yellowing bath,
rub with a solution of salt and turpentine. Rinse well.

To remove dark stains from well water in a toilet or sink,

sprinkle some citrus drink powder and swirl around. Let stand for a few minutes, then rinse.

Alternatively,

place a denture-cleaning tablet into a dirty bowl and give it a quick brushing while it fizzes away.

When you've cleaned your toilet do the water tank in the same way

– swish around toilet bowl cleaner and rinse until the water runs clear.

Dripping taps can cause a stain on the bath or sink enamel.

Try rubbing the mark with a cut lemon to get rid of it.

Fabric

'I did not mean to abuse the cloth ...'
Henry Fielding

Avoid a water stain on silk
> by placing a dry cloth underneath and
> dabbing the spot with a damp cloth.

To remove bad stains from leather,
> use wood bleach.

To remove any grease stains or oil stains
> on your clothes, coat the stain with lard.
> This will soften out the oil stain and
> make it easier to treat.

**If a mucky iron has left a stain on your
clothes,**
> cover the mark with salt, add a squeeze
> of lemon juice and leave it to rest for an
> hour. Rinse and repeat if necessary.

To get an old black grease stain off fabric,
> rub gently with margarine and then wash
> as normal.

The secret to removing blood stains on white fabric

is to use cold water and a little detergent. You can dab the stain with hydrogen peroxide, but be careful. Then rub on the secret weapon: unseasoned meat tenderizer. Rinse and wash. Do not use warm water – it will set the stain.

One way to get blood stains out of clothes

is to get the person whose blood it is to suck it off. Their own saliva should dissolve the blood. Tell that to Dracula!

Tar on washable material can be removed by rubbing with lard or butter

Scrape off any loose tar after an hour, then wash in soapy water.

If your tablecloth is stained

and you've got guests arriving any minute – don't panic! Scatter some rose or flower petals onto the cloth for an effective and pretty solution.

To remove ink stains from all sorts of materials,

spray with hairspray first.

Remove lipstick stains from linen napkins
by applying petroleum jelly before washing.

Remove chocolate stains
with a mixture of equal parts of borax powder and glycerin. Stretch the fabric over a bowl, dab the mixture on, leave for a few minutes and then wash off.

To remove grass stains,
place a clean cloth under the material and dab another cloth in methylated spirits. Clean the stain with small circular movements, working from the centre outwards.

Milk-stained clothes should be rinsed in cool water,
then washed in cold water using liquid detergent.

Remove fresh coffee stains
by applying a mixture of egg yolk and glycerin to the area. Wash out with warm water.

Remove ballpoint ink from garments
with a pencil rubber using circular movements.

For red wine,
sprinkle the fresh stain liberally with salt. Dunk in cold water and rub out stain before washing.

Remove stubborn stains from a felt hat by brushing with sandpaper.
If that fails, colour in the mark with an appropriatcly coloured felt-tip pen.

Paper

*'If all the earth were paper white
And all the sea were ink
T'were not enough for me to write
As my poor heart doth think.'*
John Lyly

Remove oil marks from paper
by covering with talcum powder, leaving overnight and then brushing off.

Remove brown stains from an old print
>by simply rubbing the paper with bread crumbs.

If you want to get ballpoint ink marks off a photograph,
>rub the mark with some silver polish wadding. Then rub the same spot with some cotton wool ... and the mark vanishes!

Hard Surfaces

'...to get blood out of a stone.'
Proverbial

To remove difficult, dried-on stains,
>sew a button onto the corner of the cloth you use for wiping down surfaces. Use the edge of the button to scrape off any stubborn crusty stains you come across.

Tobacco stains on walls
>can be removed by lightly scrubbing them with a soft brush dipped in a weak solution of washing-up liquid.

To remove children's crayon marks from walls,
brush with toothpaste using an old
toothbrush. Wipe the excess off
afterwards – for minty, clean walls!

Has Blu tac marked your walls?
Try dabbing a little toothpaste onto the
stain and leave to harden. Wash it off
afterwards, taking the mark with it.

To remove greasy stains from wood,
mix talcum powder with methylated
spirits into a sloppy paste. Paint on to the
stain and leave to dry. Brush off

To get rid of ink stains from furniture,
soak a piece of cotton wool in water and
cover the stain with it. The mark will be
drawn out and into the cotton wool.

Remove light stains from marble
using lemon juice or white wine vinegar.
Don't leave the juice or vinegar on the
marble for longer than two minutes.
Rinse off and repeat if necessary. Marble
stains easily, so get to work on stains as
quickly as possible.

For stubborn stains on marble,
use a solution of one part hydrogen peroxide to two parts water. Put a teaspoon of this solution onto the stain and then add a few drops of household ammonia. When the solution stops bubbling, rinse with lots of cold water. Great fun for budding Dr Frankensteins!

Remove rust and stains from plastic work tops with neat lemon juice.

Wooden work surfaces can be cleaned
using a nylon scouring pad dipped in hot water. Rub in the direction of the grain.

To clean a food-stained pan,
fill with distilled vinegar and soak for half an hour before washing in soapy water.

Remove tea and coffee stains from cups,
teapots and stainless steel spoons by soaking them in denture cleaner.

Or,

try mixing equal amounts of salt and vinegar, put in the cups and leave to soak. Rinse thoroughly.

Remove tannin stains from your teapot

– put a tablespoon of bicarbonate of soda into the teapot, add boiling water and leave to soak overnight. Rinse out and wash thoroughly.

Get rid of limescale from your kettle

– just put a cupful of vinegar in the kettle and boil it up. Rinse out thoroughly afterwards.

Starch can get stuck to the sole plate of an iron

– to remove it, run the iron over a piece of kitchen foil.

To shift limescale from a steam iron,

simply fill the water tank with cider vinegar, turn the iron to 'steam' and run it over a soft cloth for several minutes. You'll need to thoroughly rinse out the inside of your iron afterwards.

For a rusty iron

tie a piece of beeswax inside a rag and rub the iron when hot. Then rub with another rag sprinkled with salt.

To remove rust stains,

cover with salt. Rinse, then put some lemon juice over the stain. Leave for an hour and then wash away.

Chrome taps

come up a treat if you rub them with some plain flour then wash off.

Tarnish can be removed from silver cutlery

by placing the knives, forks and spoons in a saucepan with some scrunched-up silver foil and water and boiling for about ten minutes.

Alternatively,

to remove tarnish from silver cutlery, put a strip of kitchen foil in a plastic bowl and place the silver cutlery on top. Cover with hot water and add a handful of washing soda until clean. Rinse thoroughly.

Get rid of those awkward stubborn black spots from silver salt cellars

– immerse in a solution of one tablespoon of salt to 1 pint/600 ml of hot water for five minutes. Remove and wash the salt cellar; the spots will disappear.

To clean engraved silver

napkin rings or intricate handles on silver cutlery, rub in a little minty toothpaste with a soft cloth then wipe off.

When cleaning embossed or engraved silver,

use a small toothbrush to apply the polish. This will get into all the lines and curves.

Alternatively,

a cotton wool bud will do the trick.

To shine up badly tarnished brass

use a mixture of salt and vinegar and rub the tarnish off with a soft cloth.

Bring up a fabulous shine on bronze
> by wiping with a little vegetable oil on a
> soft cloth.

General Stains

....

*'For best results: wash in cold water
separately, hang dry and iron with warm
iron. For not so good results: drag behind
car through puddles, blow dry on roof rack.'*
Laundry instructions on a shirt made by Heet Korea

The best tip for removing any stain
> is to act at once.

**Ballpoint ink stains need to be removed
quickly;**
> dab them with a cotton wool bud dipped
> in methylated spirits.

For glue stains,
> saturate the spot with a vinegar-soaked
> cloth.

For crayon stains, rub lightly with a dry, soap-filled steel-wool pad.

Or use a damp cloth sprinkled with baking soda.

When using a damp cloth to sponge out a stain,
>   sponge once, wring out the cloth and dampen again. Otherwise, you're sponging the stain with a dirty cloth.

Don't use chemical cleaners on stains caused by drinks with chemicals in them
>   (e.g. orange squash or cola) because the chemicals in the cleaner may react with the chemicals in the drink.

Light stains
>   can be rubbed with a cut lemon.

For dark stains or rust,
>   make a paste with borax and the juice of one lemon and rub on the stain.

If your hands are stained,
rub with a piece of raw potato.
This works on kitchen work
tops too.

PETS AND ANIMALS

....

'All animals, except man, know that the principal business of life is to enjoy it.'
Samuel Butler

Cats

....

'Oh lovely Pussy! – Oh Pussy my love,
What a beautiful Pussy you are.'
Edward Lear

If your cat keeps weeing in the same spot in the house,

try feeding it in that place. It'll soon stop
using it as a toilet.

If your kitten has an bit of an accident,

transfer the puddle or poo to the litter
tray. This should attract the cat to it next
time it wants to go.

Clean a litter tray at least twice a day

– some cats are fastidious and don't like
'to go' if the tray isn't clean. Well, would
you go if the chain hadn't been pulled?

To empty a soiled cat-litter tray,

cut a plastic 4-pint or 2-litre milk carton
in half for use as a scoop.

Get cat hair off your furniture
> by rubbing the fabric with a scouring pad.

Dogs

....

'That indefatigable and unsavoury engine of pollution, the dog.'
John Sparrow

Incontinent dogs
> can make your house smell awful. Put a bit of baking soda in their drinking water to reduce the smell of their urine.

If your dog has a *wee* accident on the carpet
> don't apply disinfectant; it reacts badly with ammonia and could leave a mark. Try using a soda siphon and keep blotting the stain until dry.

When your dog has rolled in something unpleasant,
> wash him with tomato ketchup instead of shampoo. It gets rid of the strongest smells.

Prevent your dog from walking clumps of mud into the house
    – keep his paws trimmed.

It's tricky to clean your dog's teeth.
    Make it easy by wrapping a fabric plaster round one finger and dabbing on a bit of bicarbonate of soda. Use your finger as a toothbrush.

Give your dog a good rub down
    after a wet walk. Use discarded newspapers instead of towels.

Small Animals

'All animals are equal, but some are more equal than others.'
George Orwell

During the summer months,
    drinking bottles for small animals often get covered in green algae. To get rid of it, fill the bottle with sand and water,

shake it vigorously and rinse it out thoroughly. The sand scours the algae off the glass.

Also, to clean a small-necked water bottle,
fill the bottle with a little water and a plug chain. Rattle it round for a bit until the stains come off the inside.

Stop water bottles from freezing
by adding a few drops of glycerin to the water.

To get into awkward nooks and crannies when cleaning the cage,
use an old toothbrush.

Keep flies out of cages
– hang old net curtains over the front of the cage.

To clean a hamster's cage,
fill a jam jar with sawdust, put it on its side and encourage him to explore it while you do the housework on the cage. This also works if you want to create a hamster loo in one corner of the cage.

To groom your long-haired hamster,
use an old comb or toothbrush.

Wooden cages are hard to keep clean.
Gerbils also tend to chew large bits off,
so stick to a metal cage.

Stop sawdust from getting everywhere.
Stand the hutch in a cardboard box with
the sides cut down. The sawdust collects
in the bottom of the box and can be
shaken out every few days.

Horses

*'You may have my husband but not
my horse.'*
D. H. Lawrence

Saddle racks can quickly mark saddles,
so glue a couple of pieces of foam onto
the racks to protect expensive tack.

Make saddle soap go further
– melt it down in some milk before using.

Don't make your saddle too slippery
when polishing it, clean the straps and underneath but never the top part where you actually sit.

Soak a new pair of boots
in manure overnight. It will draw out any excess grease and they'll stay easier to clean.

Get a great shine on your boots
without too much elbow grease. Polish them with washing-up liquid and leave overnight.

Alternatively,
furniture polish will shine boots. For extra sparkle, try a final rub down with some nylon tights.

For a really rich shine
on boots, the penultimate layer of polish on black boots should be brown.

To harden up new boots,
add a few drops of methylated spirits to the water when first cleaning.

Keep your grip when riding

– don't polish the inside of your boots.

Buff up your velvet hat

by leaving it in the bathroom when you take a hot, steamy shower.

Keep your hoof pick clean

just ask your vet for an old syringe holder to keep it in.

To muck out,

you don't really need an expensive shovel and broom. The side of your foot and an old washing basket is just as good.

When washing greys,

for that whiter than white tail, use a blue rinse shampoo.

To keep a horse's tail shiny and tangle-free

put a little baby oil in some water and spray onto the tail. Run your fingers through to the tips.

To take the sweat off a horse,

try winding some bail twine around your hand; it makes a great scraper and you'll be able to get into all the curves of a horse's body.

If your horse gets really greasy,

he can be difficult to clean. Dip a towel in some methylated spirits and hot water, and wipe over; this will draw the grease from his coat.

Birds

'Fine feathers make fine birds.'
Proverbial

It's easy to clean your bird's cage

if you keep it lined with newspaper. Just take out the dirty sheet and replace it with a clean one.

Spruce up your parrot

– spray him once a week with lukewarm water, first thing in the morning.

If your parrot doesn't like being sprayed,
> place a container of water in the cage and
> let him bathe when he feels like it.

Fish

'A woman needs a man like a fish needs a bicycle.'
Gloria Steinem

Purify the water in a tank
> by putting watercress in the filter
> chamber. But buy it ready-prepared from
> a supermarket or grocers. If you introduce
> it from the wild, you run the risk of
> introducing diseases into the water.

To remove blanket weed from the side of a pond,
> use a windscreen ice scraper.

When cleaning out your fish tank,
> don't throw away the water. Put it on
> your garden instead. It's full of nitrates
> that will do your plants a lot of good.

To clean a tank,
remove one-third of the water every
fortnight, replacing it with clean water.

Don't situate your pond underneath trees
because you'll have your hands full
keeping the surface clear of falling leaves.

Unwelcome Pests

*'If ants are such busy workers, how come
they find time to go to all the picnics.'*
Marie Dressler

**The most effective weapon against
unwelcome creepy crawlies**
is the vacuum cleaner. Use it regularly
and make sure you always clean under
the furniture.

Bed bugs love a cosy bed

so contrary to everything your mother told you, don't make the bed! Simply leave the bedclothes folded back down and the bugs will leave in search of a warmer home.

If you suffer from asthma,

pop your pillow in the tumble dryer for 20 minutes on a hot setting to kill off any bed mites that might be lurking there.

Entice slugs from your drain

– pour some turpentine down the drain. The slugs will come out and you can get rid of them permanently.

CLOTHES

. . . .

'the apparel oft proclaims the man ...'
William Shakespeare

Washing

'*Always washing and never getting finished.*'
Thomas Hardy

Minimize the amount of detergent you use,
always place it in a detergent ball so
that it gets right into the wash and isn't
wasted in the system.

Don't ruin your best clothes in the wash.
Zips, buttons, hooks and eyes, and
poppers may cause damage to other
items, so do them up first.

Left-over detergent in fabric will attract dirt.
Use slightly less than the manufacturer's
recommended amount and if you think
there's some left in the clothes after
rinsing, give them an extra rinse.

**If you're pushed for time and don't have a
chance to mend tears**
and sew on loose buttons, put garments in
a pillowcase so they don't tear further in
the wash.

For the best wash results,
>   mix small and large items together so
>   that items can move more freely during
>   the wash.

Too many suds
>   when hand washing? Sprinkle talcum
>   powder onto the suds.

Wash silk garments after every wear,
>   or perspiration stains may be impossible
>   to remove and will actually weaken the
>   fabric.

To prevent soap scum,
>   add a tablespoon of white vinegar to the
>   rinsing water.

Really grimy work clothes?
>   Empty a can of cola onto them, add
>   detergent and run through your regular
>   wash cycle. You can try this on heavy-
>   duty clothes of any colour.

**Dirty rings on shirt collars can be removed
with oily hair shampoo,**
>   the principle is the same.

For sweaty stains spray with vinegar before washing.

As an extra measure on ground in sweat, you can also add a couple of crushed aspirin tablets into the washing water.

White cotton socks gone a bit grey? Add a slice of lemon to the water and boil them for five minutes to restore whiteness.

For really clean clothes make sure your washing machine is clean. Fill the washer of your twin tub with warm water and pour in 1 gallon/4.5 litres of distilled vinegar. Run through an entire cycle. The vinegar cleans the hoses and removes any soap scum.

If your machine overflows from too many suds, adding some fabric conditioner will get rid of the suds.

Add one cup of white vinegar to the final rinse cycle to eliminate lint.

Instead of using expensive sheets of fabric conditioner,

add a few capfuls of liquid fabric conditioner and water to a bowl, swish a washcloth around in the mixture, ring out the cloth and toss into the dryer.

Rinse washable wool garments in lukewarm water

and add a few tablespoons of glycerin to keep them soft. It also helps prevent itching.

Stop tights and stockings from getting in a tangle

during washing. Place them in an old pillowcase or cushion cover. This works for delicate items as well.

Make a 'delicates' bag

for the washing machine out of old net curtains.

To stop your tights from laddering,

starch the tights lightly before you wash them.

Put your woollies in a pillowcase

to spin dry them without losing their shape.

When washing silk,

a couple of lumps of sugar added to the final rinse will give the silk more body and make life all the sweeter.

If your jumper's cuffs go baggy

after washing, try dipping them in cold water then drying them with a very hot hair-dryer – they should shrink back to shape.

Wash your clothes pegs

once in a while by putting them inside a pillowcase in the machine. Then they won't leave dirty marks on clean washing.

When soaking an item of clothing

to remove a stain, always immerse the whole garment to avoid patchiness even if the stain itself is only small.

If you don't want your jeans to fade
when washed, soak them in a water and vinegar solution before you first wear them.

If you're unsure whether a coloured garment will run,
pop a white hanky in with the load to pick up any dye. When the hanky stays white, you're safe to wash these clothes with your whites.

Alternatively, to check whether an item is colourfast
when dry, iron a corner of it between two white cloths. If any dye runs, you'll know it needs to be washed separately.

Cut down on creases when washing a sari
– fold it up and place it in a pillowcase before putting in to the wash.

Wetsuits can pong if not looked after
– keep yours in top condition by always rinsing inside and out with fresh water after use.

Get rid of wetsuit smells
by rinsing the suit with disinfectant solution on a regular basis.

Drying

'Many a good hanging prevents a bad marriage.'
William Shakespeare

A cost effective way of drying clothes
is to put a dry towel in with the tumble-dry clothes. This will absorb moisture and reduce the drying time.

Rolling wet clothes
in a towel before tumble drying is another energy-saving alternative.

Clean out the lint filter in your drier after every use.

When hanging clothes outside to dry,
try to avoid direct sunlight. If that's
impossible, turn them inside out to avoid
colour fading.

A dirty washing line may leave dirty marks
on your lovely clean washing … avoid
the problem by wrapping a soft sponge
around the line and pulling it along the
full length every so often.

**Especially before hanging your clean sheets
over a washing line,**
clean the line with a damp cloth or you'll
get a grubby line across the sheet.

Save space on your washing line,
peg your socks or smalls onto a wire
hanger and hang that from the line.

Hang a clean white wet shirt outside
on a cold morning and it will come up
bright white.

Turn white T-shirts and shirts inside out
and dry in the shade if possible so that
direct sunlight doesn't turn them yellow.

To ensure the pleats stay in a pleated skirt
while it's drying on a washing line, hang by the waistband (dry all skirts by the waistband) and clip a clothes peg to the bottom of the pleats.

When drying socks on a line,
they should be pegged by the heels because this keeps the stretch in the right direction.

Throw nylon netting in the drier to catch any excess lint.

To treat the worst lint-attracting offender, corduroy,
brush it with a clothes brush while still damp.

If you're drying a dark T-shirt over a clothes horse,
turn it inside out so that you don't get a line across the T-shirt.

Leave dry-cleaning plastic bags on the wire hangers

and use when drip-drying shirts. The shirts won't stick together, and so will dry a lot quicker.

Ironing

'To the question "Who wears the pants in this house?" I reply "I do, and I also wash and iron them."'
Denis Thatcher

Reduce your ironing load

after washing T-shirts and sweat shirts. Fold carefully when still slightly damp and dry in a warm place. They won't need any ironing.

Start your ironing with items that need a cool iron.

Gradually work through the ironing, working up to items that need a hotter setting.

If your pile of ironing has become too dry,
pop it back into the tumble drier with
a wet towel for a minute. This will get
the clothes slightly damp again and easy
to iron. If you don't have a tumble drier,
wrap them in a wet towel instead.

To remove fabric shine,
dampen a cloth and wring out the excess
water. Put this cloth on top of the shiny
fabric and steam press. Do this several
times, pressing the area almost dry.

When ironing velvet,
fold a thick towel in two and place over
the reverse side of the velvet before using
the iron.

To put a good, lasting crease in trousers,
apply a thin line of paper glue along the
inside of the crease, then iron.

When ironing the collar of a shirt,
go from one tip to the middle and then
repeat. Never iron straight across the
collar because this pushes the fibre
across to one end and makes the collar
uneven.

Ironing on the reverse side
of clothes keeps the colour longer.

Protect delicate buttons
when ironing – place a metal spoon over
them.

Avoid ironing silk and velvet altogether
they will lose their creases if hung in a
steamy bathroom.

Clean the bottom of your iron
with wet wipes.

Iron dark clothes inside out
to stop heat lines.

To avoid marking a hat when ironing
always use a chromium-plated iron.

If your iron sticks to your clothes,
wrap a bar of soap in a hanky and rub
it over the hot face of the iron – it will
soon be as smooth as new.

When ironing non-delicate fabrics
put a drop of essential oil into your
steam iron water to make clothes smell
nice.

When ironing bed linen,
spray it with with water infused with
lavender oil. The smell will help you
sleep.

**After ironing, fold matching sheets and duvet
covers**
and place inside matching pillowcases.
This way, sets will be much easier to
find.

General

'Give me a laundry list and I will set it
to music.'
Rossini

Stop dirty clothes from becoming too overpowering;

an empty perfume bottle at the bottom of
a laundry bag keeps things sweet.

For rust marks on cotton apply lemon juice and salt,

then let dry in the sun.

On white garments, cover rust stains

with cream of tartar and gather up the
ends of the garment to keep the powder
on the stain. Dip the spot into hot water
for five minutes, then wash as usual.

Shoe polish on your trousers?

Apply one part rubbing alcohol and two
parts water on coloured fabrics. Use
straight alcohol on whites.

To remove rain spots from suede,
rub lightly with an emery board.

To remove grease spots from suede,
dip a cloth in vinegar and blot out the
stain. Brush with a suede brush to restore
the nap.

Instead of using bleach,
leave newly washed clothes out in the
sun to dry; the sun acts as a natural
bleach.

**Keep tough stains away from hot water or
steam.**
Lots of foods contain albumen, a protein
which is fixed by heat, so tackle the
stain before putting in a hot wash, for
instance.

**As soon as dirt appears on your treasured
sheepskin coat**
or suede jacket, get it cleaned. Ground in
dirt will never come out.

Ballpoint ink on your best suede jacket or bag?

Very carefully, try gently rubbing an emery board or fine sandpaper on the offending mark.

If you get blood on a sheepskin coat,

sprinkle potting compost on it and leave overnight. It works like blotting paper. Just brush it off in the morning.

To prevent mildew,

ensure clothes are dried thoroughly after washing.

Use wet wipes to clean patent leather

or bring a shine to your PVC trousers!

To make tights and stockings last longer,

wet them thoroughly, wring out the excess water and then freeze them in a plastic bag. When you want to wear them, thaw them out and dry them thoroughly.

White line down your jeans?

Mix some permanent blue ink with water until you've got the right shade. Paint down the line with a small brush and leave the jeans to dry.

Make sure you don't spray eau-de-Cologne on your tie

– it'll damage the material.

Wear ties alternately.

Ties spring back into shape when they get a rest between wearings.

Dirty marks on white material

can be covered up with white chalk.

Remove pencil marks from embroidery material

by rubbing the fabric with white bread kneaded into a ball.

Protect your wedding dress

– sew two cotton sheets together as a protective cover.

Just got back from the pub? Clothes smell of smoke?
Put them in the tumble drier with a fabric conditioner sheet for five minutes and they'll come out smelling as fresh as a daisy.

Hats

'No-one knows how ungentlemanly he can look until he has seen himself in a shocking bad hat.'
R.S. Surtees

To prevent your hats becoming discoloured,
use acid-free tissue paper to store them.

To clean a Panama hat,
wipe it with a mixture of water and lemon juice and a soft clean cloth.

To get marks off your Panama hat,
rub them with stale bread.

Brush your felt hat

gently with a soft brush after each wear.
Keep it in a plastic bag when you're not
wearing it.

If you get caught in the rain wearing a felt hat,

use tissue paper to blot the raindrops
away and then get a handful of tissue
paper and run it over the hat with a
smooth circular action.

If your felt hat has become droopy,

steam it for a few seconds and then brush
it gently, making sure you are brushing
in the direction of the nap.

To bring up the colour on a white or cream felt hat,

sprinkle with talcum powder.

Alternatively,

sprinkle a white or cream felt hat with
bran. Leave it over night and then brush
it off in the morning. It works like an
exfoliater.

When steaming a hat,

use a kettle with a short spout not a jug kettle. You'll have more control over the direction of the steam.

To revive flowers on a hat,

shake them over a steaming kettle and they'll blossom back into life.

Clean a felt hat

by wrapping sticky tape round your hand and gently dabbing the fluff away.

Alternatively,

brush a felt hat vigorously with a nail brush and then steam over a kettle to bring the pile back up.

Shoes

'I kiss his dirty shoe ... '
William Shakespeare

To clean the white rubber areas
(the 'bumpers') on training shoes, use toothpaste.

To clean white training shoes,
rub with bathroom cleaner, buff and then wipe off with a rag.

Alternatively,
use cheap face cleansing milk.

Scuffs on high heels or shoes
can be covered up using magic marker or felt-tip pen.

Satin wedding shoes often get ruined because of water marks.
Remove the stains by dipping some cotton wool in a little white spirit and

dabbing it over the shoe. If the shoe is brightly dyed satin, test a small area inside first before trying this.

Wedding shoes come in such subtle colours

it can be hard to find a match for your outfit. Try rubbing oil pastels over the shoes; these come in a full spectrum of shades. When you find the perfect match, seal the shoes with a little neutral polish.

Dyed shoes often mark your feet when they get wet.

Prevent this from happening by spraying the inside of the shoe with some Scotchguard.

Bring the shine back to patent leather

– rub a little vegetable or baby oil over the shoe and then buff with some kitchen paper towel.

Alternatively,

patent leather will sparkle after polishing with furniture polish.

Scuff marks can be covered up
by gently building up layers of felt-tip
pens until you reach the perfect colour
match.

Even the grubbiest of trainers
look fit for Centre Court if you give them
a good clean with a baby wipe.

**Keep new trainers looking white for as long as
possible**
– spray them with starch when you get
them home from the shops. This makes
them easier to clean as well.

If you've got marks on your white stilettos,
try getting rid of them with nail varnish
remover. If you can't get them off, dab
some correction fluid over the marks.

Remove black marks from white leather shoes
by gently rubbing with a damp scouring
pad.

Get rid of black spots on white shoes and handbags

with nail-varnish remover.

White leather shoes

appreciate a wipe down with beaten egg white instead of polish. Use cotton wool to clean them and then polish with a soft cloth.

Stiletto heels always get scuffed and marked.

Try spraying them with some matching car paint as a tough and durable solution.

Clean wooden heels

with furniture polish.

To keep your football boots in good condition,

avoid products that have paraffin in them because this will rot the leather.

Never wear new leather shoes in the rain.

They need a bit of wear and tear to build up water resistance.

For an effective waterproof coating,
give your shoes a final polish with a coat
of floor wax.

If you've run out of shoe polish,
you can use a little floor wax, furniture
polish or window-cleaning spray.

For an alternative brown shoe polish,
rub the inside of a banana skin along the
leather. Leave shoes to dry and don't buff
them up.

For black shoes,
polish with the inside of the rind of a
fresh orange.

To give shoes an instant antique look,
buy them one shade lighter than you
really want but clean them with a
slightly darker polish.

If your shoes get soaked,
take them off as soon as you get home
and stuff with newspaper. Leave them to
dry out naturally; don't try to speed the

process up by putting them in front of a fire or in bright sunshine. When they are dry, use some saddle soap to condition them and then polish.

To keep shoes smelling sweet,
fill a fine plant spray with water and some eau-de-Cologne and give the shoes a little shower.

If you have smelly feet,
sprinkle some bicarbonate of soda in your shoes overnight to cut down on the pong.

Or, place orange peel in a pair of smelly summer shoes
overnight and they'll be much fresher next day.

Or, you could try placing a sheet of fabric conditioner in them.

Alternatively,
>   deodorize trainers by filling the feet of
>   pop socks with unused cat litter, tie the
>   ends, place inside the trainers and leave
>   overnight.

Patent leather shoes come up a treat
>   if rubbed over with petroleum jelly.

Canvas shoes
>   often look grubby very quickly. Carpet
>   shampoo, applied with a small brush,
>   will make them look as good as new.

Prevent your shoes from scuffing
>   by painting a layer of clear nail varnish
>   on to the heel and toe of your shoes.

Wardrobes

'They look quite promising in the shops, and not entirely without hope when I get them back into my wardrobe. But then, when I put them on they tend to deteriorate with a very strange rapidity and one feels so sorry for them.'
Joyce Grenfell on clothes

If you're worried about damp in your cupboards,

tie a handful of sticks of chalk together and hang them inside. They will absorb any moisture.

Moths don't like

bay leaves, allspice berries or cedar chips, so put some in your wardrobes.

Also to keep moths away,

place conkers in your wardrobes and drawers.

Make your own pomander

by sticking whole cloves into the skin of an orange. Then place a teaspoon of ground cinnamon and a teaspoon of orris root in a plastic bag along with the studded orange. Shake until it's coated all over. Store the orange in tissue paper for at least two weeks before hanging in your wardrobe.

To freshen in wardrobes and cupboards,

use a sheet of fabric conditioner in among the clothes.

Absorb smells in any closed closet

– charcoal bricks placed in a small muslin sack will absorb the pong – ideal for families with teenage boys!

Hang ties in a wardrobe with the 'good' side facing inwards

to keep them dust free.

PERSONAL GROOMING

'If I'd known I was gonna live this long
I'd have taken better care of myself.'
Eubie Blake

General

....

'Even I don't wake up looking like Cindy Crawford.'
Cindy Crawford

To stop flecks of toothpaste getting on your clothes while you're cleaning your teeth,
wrap a towel around your shoulders to cover your front.

Prevent cosmetic bottles from spilling
when travelling – dab a little nail varnish around the edges of the caps to seal them tightly.

Face flannels can be thoroughly sterilized
by placing them in a microwave while still damp and 'cooking' for five minutes.

Don't buy soap.
Use natural oatmeal – it works just as well.

Avoid bubbles in your nail varnish
– gently roll the bottle to mix it rather than shake it up as usual.

Remove any stains left by nail varnish
by dipping your nails into fresh lemon juice.

Remove dead skin and beat facial blackheads
by adding a teaspoon of sugar to your palms when you wash your face and lathering it up with soap.

To remove blackheads,
apply gentle pressure to the affected area with the rounded end of a hair grip.

To get rid of spots,
mix three teaspoons of honey with one teaspoon of cinnamon and dab onto your face nightly. In two weeks you'll have really clear skin.

No shaving foam?
Use peanut butter if you don't have anything else.

Alternatively,
> smear on some olive oil.

Take your shower or bath before you shave
> to soften up the bristles. If you don't
> have time for full ablutions, try pressing
> a warm flannel against your stubble
> instead.

Don't put shaving foam all over your brush
> because you'll end up with far too much.
> Instead, separate the bristles and put a bit
> of foam inside and then close the bristles
> round the foam. This way, you'll get the
> little bit you need gently released as you
> shave.

After shaving,
> rinse thoroughly in cold water to close
> up your pores.

For baby smooth skin,
> add a cupful of milk granules to your
> bath and enjoy a long soak.

For a sensuous bath,
mix a few drops of your favourite
perfume in with some good olive oil.

Here's a fruity way to get rid of ugly verrucas
– wrap a banana skin around your foot,
with the inside of the skin against your
foot. You could hold it in place with a
sock over the top. Repeat nightly for four
weeks and the offending verruca will
disappear.

**Don't waste your money on expensive facial
water sprays**
– just use a regular plant spray bottle
filled with some mineral water. It's great
for hot days and sets make-up a treat.

If your eyelids are sticky in the morning,
dip a cotton bud in baby shampoo –
which doesn't sting – and use it to clean
the roots of your lashes. Then wash your
eyes in clear cool water.

If your eyes are puffy after washing,
apply the pulp of a roasted apple to your
eyelids.

To exfoliate and soften hands,
work a mixture of olive oil and granulated sugar into them, then rinse off.

To give yourself a good back scrub,
place a bar of soap about half-way down a stocking leg. Tie a knot on each side of the soap and hold one end of the stocking in each hand. With a seesawing motion scrub your back. For a more vigorous scrub use grainy exfoliating soap.

Run out of toothpaste?
A little bit of bicarbonate of soda does the trick.

For a cheap moisturiser,
blend a banana with a little milk and smooth onto your face for twenty minutes then wipe off.

If you have excess moisturiser on your hands,
don't rinse it off, run your fingers through your hair – the cream will prevent frizz and makes a good conditioner.

There's no need to buy expensive make-up removers
　– baby oil does the job brilliantly.

Or,
　　try using cold milk.

Smelly feet?
　　Try rubbing in a little eucalyptus oil.

Or,
　　sprinkle some talc inside your socks to
　　keep them dry and smelling sweet.

Nobody likes bad breath . . .
　　chew on a little garden mint.

Try cleansing your mouth
　　with fennel or aniseed seeds available
　　from health food shops. Chew them after
　　meals to get best results.

Chewing parsley leaves
　　as often as you can throughout the day
　　will also keep your breath fresh and
　　works especially well on garlic smells.

To help cure bad breath,
drink diluted aloe vera juice – just add
several dessertspoons to a glass of water.

Freshen up bad breath instantly
by chewing two or three sprigs of
watercress and a couple of grapes.

Soak dentures overnight in white vinegar
and brush with a toothbrush.

To save water,
clean your teeth using a mug rather than
have the water running constantly.

Also,
replace one bath with a shower each
week.

Fingers that have become superglued
together can be unstuck by rolling a
pencil gently between them.

If you are unfortunate enough to have superglued your eyelids together,
> don't despair. A damp cotton wool pad held over the eye should do the trick.

To keep spectacles clean,
> rinse them in clear water every morning.

Hair

'She would never get married because you couldn't wear curlers in bed.'
Edna O'Brien

Body shampoo is just as good as hair shampoo
> – and half the price.

Make your own egg shampoo by mixing two eggs and half an eggshell of olive oil.
> Just massage into your scalp and rinse thoroughly.

If you run out of hair conditioner,
> fabric conditioner will do just as well.

Don't pile long hair on top of your head when washing.

It will make it tangle. Instead wash hair hanging straight down.

Olive oil makes a fabulous conditioner.

Rub a little through dry hair then wrap your hair in a warm towel for ten minutes. Shampoo out.

Detangle knotty hair

– just comb some lemonade through it.

After a dye job,

cotton wool dipped in milk rubbed onto your skin will remove any stains.

To ease itching caused by dandruff or a dry scalp,

soak some dried thyme and sage in warm water and then use it as a final rinse.

Don't buy expensive dandruff shampoos

– just add a little olive oil to your conditioner.

Alternatively, if you suffer from dandruff,
place one teaspoon of parsley and an egg
in a cup and beat together. Massage into
your hair, leave for five minutes, then
rinse out thoroughly.

Another good cure for dandruff
is to put about 10 or 12 stinging nettle
heads into a bowl. Pour boiling water
over them and leave to cool. Strain so
that any bits are removed. The left-over
liquid can be used as a final rinse after
shampooing.

To stop dandruff from proliferating,
soak your comb in vinegar.

Hair is more fragile when wet,
so be careful when brushing after
washing. Using a wide-toothed comb
helps to minimize the damage.

Heal and prevent split ends
by rubbing corn oil into your hair,
making sure the ends are covered. Leave
on for several minutes and then rinse.

Remember to wash your hairbrushes and combs as well.

Add a capful of shampoo to warm water, wash and rinse.

Herbal

'Well, now, there's a remedy for everything...'
Cervantes

For a bath-time treat,

make your own herbal infusion. Put dried herbs in a muslin bag (you can use fresh herbs but they're not as concentrated as dried ones), tie it to the hot water tap so that the water flows over and through the bag. When the bath is ready, put the bag in the water and leave it to float around while you bathe.

For a reviving bath,

use herbs such as mint (to stimulate), nettles (to boost circulation), pine (which is refreshing) and thyme (which has antiseptic qualities).

For a relaxing bath,

use lavender. Marjoram is a great natural tranquillizer, sage is an antidote for stress and lemon balm relieves tension.

To get rid of warts,

rub them with the milky sap from a dandelion stalk.

Combat acne

with some comfrey or marigold ointment. Dabbing on lemon juice and garlic also helps dry up spots.

An alternative antiseptic cream

can be made from thyme leaves, scraped off the stem and then crushed on a board. Apply this paste to the affected area.

Make your own toothpaste.

Take some juniper twigs and leaves when the sap is full. Dry them in the airing cupboard. Place them in a large metal tray and set fire to them. The resulting ash can be used to clean your teeth.

Babies

'The sweetest smell ... and also the most foul.'
Anon.

Don't be too fastidious

by constantly washing and changing the cot sheets – babies like the smell of familiar surroundings.

Bathing tiny babies can be a bit tricky.

You may find it easier to bathe them in a sink rather than be bending down over a large tub. Cover the sink taps with a towel so that you don't bang the baby's head against them.

If your baby dislikes having a bath,

it may be because the room is too cold for him or her. Make sure the room is warm before you start the bath, or bathe the baby in a warm room if you can't heat the bathroom successfully.

Babies can be bathed
every day or every other day. You should
'top and tail' them – wipe their faces and
bottoms – at least twice a day.

New babies (up to a month old)
can be washed in a washing-up bowl.
Remember to cover the taps with a towel
to protect your baby's head. And remove
dirty pots and pans first!

To prevent babies from slipping in a big bath,
use a terry nappy or towel as a non-slip
mat.

Never leave a baby or child alone in the bath.
It only takes a few inches of water to
drown a child, so always supervise bath
time.

Babies quickly get cold after a bath.
Make sure you have everything you'll
need before you put your baby in the
water.

Feed a baby after a bath and not before.
Babies often decide to throw up if they've
been jiggled around, so wait until after
they've been cleaned before feeding.

Keep all your equipment together
– use a hanging shoe container which
you can fill with cotton wool, ointment,
creams, terry towels ... in fact, anything
that you need for changing or cleaning
your baby. It can be hung on a wall or
door for easy access.

Alternatively,
plastic stacking boxes from DIY stores
are cheaper than specially designed baby
equipment.

When babies are young, put them in nighties
not playsuits at night. It will make
frequent night changes easier and less
disruptive and begin to teach them the
difference between night and day.

Lay out a clean set of night clothes before you go to bed

> so that you're not stumbling around in the gloom if you have to do a complete change in the wee small hours.

Make your own baby wipes

> – they're cheaper and less synthetic. Simply soak some cotton wool roll in an old ice cream carton filled with water and a little baby oil. Tear off strips as you need it.

When you wash a child's hair,

> draw a thin line of petroleum jelly above the eyes; it will stop any of the shampoo running down into the eyes and stinging them.

Also,

> a golf visor helps keep shampoo out of a child's eyes.

Cleaning first milk teeth

is a fiddly job and many babies hate toothbrushes. Instead, wrap a little muslin around your finger – it's much easier for getting at little gnashers.

When children are cleaning their teeth,

use an egg timer in the bathroom so they know how long they should clean their teeth for.

Encourage your children to tidy their rooms

with an egg timer or clock. Make it a race with prizes for the tidiest competitor.

Children's tattoos don't always come off easily,

use a tiny drop of nail-varnish remover on a cotton bud.

If the kids are left with orange moustaches after drinking cordial

rub on some toothpaste and rinse. Lovely clean smiles!

THE GREAT OUTDOORS

'Gentlemen know that fresh air should be kept in its proper place – out of doors – and that, God having given us indoors and out-of-doors, we should not attempt to do away with this distinction.'

Rose Macaulay

Gardening

....

'... I feel quite sure that happiness is no longer a possibility. Yet when I talk to my gardener, I'm convinced of the opposite.'
Bertrand Russell

Repot a plant without making a mess.

Simply place the old pot inside the new larger pot and fill the gap with soil. Then remove the smaller pot, take the plant out of the old pot and place into the hole in the new pot.

Shift stains from plastic garden furniture

with a paste made from bicarbonate of soda and water. Leave the paste on the stain for about two minutes and then wipe off.

To preserve aluminium garden furniture

over winter, lightly wipe down with cooking oil. Remember to wipe off the oil when you want to use the furniture again.

To remove rust from garden tools,
mix two tablespoonfuls of salt with one tablespoonful of lemon juice. Apply this mixture to the rust and rub hard.

To store garden tools over winter,
grease lightly with cooking oil.

To prevent your tools from rusting,
store them in buckets of sand and oil.

Alternatively,
use any left-over engine oil. Leave the bottle to drain into a jar, then brush the oil onto your garden tools or furniture to keep them in good condition. Wipe off before using.

Put soap under your finger nails
before gardening. They'll be much easier to clean afterwards.

Get hands clean
after a hard day's gardening with soap, water and sugar.

Bring the shine back to dusty house plants
by wiping the leaves with a mixture of
milk and water.

To keep cacti dust-free,
brush gently every week with a pastry
brush.

House Exterior

'...the house allows one to dream in peace...'
Gaston Bachelard

In icy weather,
clean the doorstep with a bucketful
of water to which you have added a
crushed aspirin, 8 fl oz/250 ml of warm
water and one tablespoon of methylated
spirits. This will keep the step clean and
stop ice from forming.

Remove dirt, sand, small rock particles and debris from your entrance way
> so that it can't be tracked into the home. A simple solution that will save you time in the long run.

Unclog grease from your drains –
> pour a cup of salt water and a cup of fizzy soda into the drain followed by a pan of boiling water. The grease will usually dissolve immediately and open the drain.

For a cheap drain cleaner,
> lye – a caustic solution from hardware stores – is just as effective.

Take a water hose and spray the outside of your house.
> This will remove the dust and cobwebs. On textured walls, attach a car-washing brush to the hose to remove dirt.

For outside windows,
> dip a long-handled mop in your cleaning solution, wash the windows, then hose them off. Throw a clean towel over the mop to dry the glass.

Dry windows outside in one direction
and inside in the other direction. If you see a streak, you will know if it is inside or outside.

To keep frost off windows,
add anti-freeze to your cleaning water. Rub the inside of windows with a sponge dipped in the solution. Polish with newspapers or paper towels.

To get stains off bricks,
rub or grate the marked brick with another similar brick.

Dirty hammers
are actually dangerous – the head will keep slipping if it gets really grimy. Try banging it on a piece of wood covered with sandpaper a few times, or, alternatively, rub the head over some coarse sand.

To remove barbecue fat stains from your patio,
cover with cat litter, grind with your heel, leave for some time and later just sweep up.

Keep barbecue grills clean by leaving the grill over the heat after cooking for 20 minutes or so.

For gas-run barbecues set to the highest setting, for charcoal just use the left-over coals. Finish by rubbing over with a wire brush.

To remove food stuck on barbecue racks,

leave them out overnight on the grass. The dew will soften the food, making them easier to clean.

To keep your barbecue clean,

line it with a double layer of aluminium foil. It's then easier to remove the ashes, and leaves no messy charcoal resin.

To clean perspex and get rid of scratches,

rub with toothpaste and then buff up with a cloth.

Fishing

....

*'An angler is a man who spends his
rainy days sitting around on muddy
banks because his wife won't let him
do it at home.'*
The Irish Times

Store fishing lines in a dark place
    because UV light damages them.

Clean fishing rods with white spirit.

Rinse and dry fishing nets out after each use,
    otherwise they'll rot.

**Rinse and hang your waders up to dry straight
and upside down.**
    This will prevent kinks that would make
    them fracture.

Also, rub in olive oil to prevent cracking.

**The sooner you pare a fish after catching it,
the less mess you'll make.**

Use polish on fishing rods
    to make them water-repellent.

Stop fishing hooks going rusty,
    put a couple of drops of vegetable oil in
    the box with them.

Soak fishing lines after use in washing-up liquid
    to stop them going rusty.

Football

'Ossie Ardiles was the difference. It was
like trying to tackle dust.'
Joe Royle

Stop studs rusting into the soles of football boots,
    unscrew them and rub petroleum jelly on
    to the screw before screwing back in.

Never tumble dry football shirts with names and numbers on the back
    – you'll melt the transfers.

Hang football shirts on your wall between washings and wearings
– they make great posters.

Don't knock mud off the soles of football boots by banging them against a wall
– you'll damage both the wall and the studs. Instead, leave the mud to dry and then peel it off.

Many football boots – despite appearances – aren't actually made of leather, but are synthetic.
Avoid the hassle of polishing – synthetic boots can be cleaned with soapy water.

Contrary to popular belief, use shoe polish on leather football boots rather than dubbin.
Dubbin stops the leather breathing.

Leave leather boots to dry in a cool place
– drying them under a radiator or in an airing cupboard will dry out the oils in the leather and it'll crack.

When folding up football shirts after washing,
avoid folding along the line of the
sponsor's name on the front of the shirt –
you'll crack the print!

If your team has two kits,
wear them alternately to get the life back
into them between matches.

**The best thing to clean white stripes on
football boots is a bit of kitchen-cleaner
cream.**
Second best is toothpaste.

**And the best way to touch up trendy coloured
boots is with a simple crayon of the right
colour.**

To air sweaty, smelly goalkeeper's gloves,
turn them inside out and attach them
to the handle-bars of a bike with rubber
bands. Then ride round on the bike!

Golf

....

*'Tee the ball high. Because years of
experience have shown me that air offers
less resistance than dirt.'*
Jack Niklaus

**Your gloves should be kept in mint condition
at all times.**
> Golf gloves are made from first class
> leather and cost a lot of money, so keep
> them in a small plastic bag when not in
> use.

To clean the grooves in your clubs,
> use an old toothbrush.

Smart wooden clubs can soon look shoddy
> when the paint becomes chipped. Instead
> of buying expensive paints, try applying
> two layers of permanent marker pen –
> first black, then red – which together
> make a lovely deep brown. Seal with a
> varnish and your clubs will look the part
> for ages.

Travel

....

'If you look like your passport picture,
you're too ill to travel.'
Will Kommen

Before going off on holiday,
   leave half a lemon in each of your rooms
   at home to keep them smelling sweet.

Pack an empty pillowcase to pop all your dirty
clothes in whilst you're away.
   It saves time sorting the clean from the
   dirty once you're at home again.

Seal all bottles and jars with some clear nail
varnish
   to avoid messy spillages whilst
   travelling.

Caravanning

'Every woman, every man, join the caravan of love.'
The Housemartins

Prevent your caravan screen from being splattered by flies
– just cover the screen with cling film when travelling and peel it away when you stop. All the flies come away with the cling film.

If travelling during the winter,
always wash your caravan down to avoid salt from the road corroding the surface.

Protect yourself from greasy stains from tow hitches,
place a split tennis ball over the towball.

Alternatively,
just pop a sock over the top of the hitch when you've parked.

Save money – don't buy a caravan toilet brush
> – just get a washing-up brush and place it
> in a plastic beaker.

Camping

....

'Camping is just one canned thing
after another.'
Peggy Edmunds

Toothbrushes quickly get mucky,
> so cut one down and keep it in a film
> canister.

Alternatively,
> cover the head of your toothbrush with
> some foil when not in use.

Keep your soap clean
> – store it in the foot of some tights slung
> over a nearby tree.

Colour code stuff sacks
> so that you know which is dirty washing,
> where your clean clothes are, which

bag has your smalls or wet weather gear and so on.

Make the washing up easier
– coat the outside of your pan with diluted soapy liquid before you begin cooking.

Alternatively,
if you don't have soapy liquid, try a generous coating of mud.

For stubborn food deposits,
try rubbing with a clump of grass.

Also,
a scrunched-up piece of kitchen foil makes a good pot scourer.

Take small, easily stored amounts of washing-up liquid
in eye drop containers or film canisters.

Avoid as much washing up as possible
– take boil-in-the-bag food.

To get rid of stale, nasty smells from a water carrier,
fill with water and drop a denture-cleaning tablet in. Leave for a couple of hours and then rinse out thoroughly.

Get rid of smells from your Thermos flask
by adding a denture-cleaning tablet and some water. Leave to soak for 20 minutes, then rinse thoroughly and drain.

Alternatively,
fill the flask with water and one tablespoon of bicarbonate of soda. Leave to soak. Rinse and drain.

To clean brushes in the great outdoors when you're painting,
fill empty film canisters with white spirit.

TRANSPORT

···

*'They say travel broadens the mind;
but you must have the mind.'*
G. K. Chesterton

Cars

....

'I think that cars truly are almost the exact equivalent of the great Gothic cathedrals.'
Roland Barthes

Leaks in your engine
are a lot easier to spot and fix if the engine is free of grease and grime.

While you're cleaning under your bonnet, it's a great time to look at all hoses, wires, belts, etc.
Check the hoses for cracks, or spongy or soft spots.

To clean your car windows,
partly roll them down, clean the top edges and next to the rubber gaskets first. As these are the dirtiest parts of the window, clean them with a separate cloth before you tackle the main part of the glass.

Spray glass cleaner on your cloth,

and not on the glass itself to avoid overspray on the vehicle's painted surfaces.

To avoid scratches on paintwork when cleaning car windows,

get rid of chunky belt buckles and don't wear jeans with rivets or studs.

Always wipe parallel to heated rear window lines.

If you rub vigorously in the wrong direction, you risk catching on any cuts in the film and tearing it.

Clean one wheel at a time.

Don't run around the vehicle trying to keep each wheel at the same stage of cleaning as cleaners shouldn't be allowed to dry, or remain on the wheels any longer than the instructions state.

To avoid any overspray of cleaning products from tyre to hub caps,

cut out a cardboard disc the same size as the hub caps, with two horizontal slots

for your finger and thumb. For extra
strength, cover the disc with tape to
stop any liquid from seeping through the
cardboard. Place the disc over the hub
cap to protect it while you're cleaning
each tyre in turn.

Use a nylon scrub brush to remove dirt from heavily grained vinyl soft tops.

Be careful not to get the brush or the
cleaner on the vehicle's paint.

Don't apply vinyl and rubber protectants to your windscreen wiper blades.

It makes them less effective.

Remember, cleaning your car is just like cleaning your house.

Tidy up first, then vacuum, followed
by carpet cleaning, upholstery cleaning,
dashboard cleaning and any small
interior detailing you care to do, such as
cleaning glass and chrome surfaces.

To speed up the drying process after cleaning your car,

leave your doors open, but make sure you shut off the interior lights by sticking something in the door jamb that keeps the buttons closed, or disconnecting the battery.

Before using shop-bought stain remover

or a home-made version of upholstery or carpet shampoo on your vehicle's interior, first test it on an inconspicuous area, such as under the seat, to make sure it won't remove the colour from the material.

To remove sticky sweets or chocolate from car upholstery,

use a cloth soaked in lukewarm water and blot and wipe until the stain is removed.

Crayon, oil or grease can be removed from car seats

by scraping off any excess with a blunt knife blade first, then blotting with a paper towel. If needed, a stain remover can be used afterwards.

Coffee, fruit, ice cream and milk stains

can be rubbed with a cloth soaked in cold water, but don't use soap as this may set the stain.

Sponge urine stains with lukewarm mild soapsuds;

rinse with a cloth soaked in cold water, then soak a cloth in a solution of one part ammonia to five parts water. Hold it on the stain for one minute and then rinse with a clean, wet cloth.

Sponge vomit with a clean cloth dipped in cold water.

Wash lightly with lukewarm water and mild soap. If the odour persists, treat with a solution of one teaspoon baking soda in one cup of warm water.

Don't use polish or cleaners on steering wheels and floor pedals.

They'll make surfaces slippery, which could lead to accidents.

Take care of your chamois leather.
Wash it in warm, soapy water and rinse it out after use. Let the leather dry away from direct heat so that the cloth keeps in the natural oils.

When washing your car,
don't use washing-up liquid because it contains salt, which can cause rust to form.

Remove rust spots from chrome bumpers.
Dip kitchen foil in cola and rub off the rust spots.

Always keep a supply of hand wipes
from fast food outlets and plastic gloves from petrol stations to keep your hands clean when you have to do any minor repairs.

Clean your windscreen
with warm water and a good dash of white vinegar.

On a cold morning

when the car window steams up, rub a
cut potato on the inside and then wipe
off the excess smear. This helps stop
condensation.

Mop up oil spills

with cat litter. Pour a thick layer over
the spill and leave for about 24 hours.
Just sweep it up when the oil has been
absorbed.

To polish your car,

use a flunky (an imitation chamois), not
a chamois leather. Never let it dry out –
keep it in a sealable plastic bag.

To get the best shine on your windscreen,

use newspaper to clean the glass.

To keep your windscreen clean,

keep a jar of baking soda and a soft cloth
in the car. When it rains, dampen the
cloth and put lots of baking soda on it;
wipe the car windows and rinse off.

To clean your chrome wheels,
use lemonade. It works a treat.

Keep your bumpers looking as good as new
– wipe them over with some petrol and
then clean with black boot polish for a
really shiny finish.

When cleaning the limousine,
use boot polish on the rubber trim of the
interior.

Buff up the windows
with newspaper and a mixture of water
and vinegar.

When you have cleaned the Rolls,
don't forget to wind the windows down
slightly and wipe off any excess water
and soap from the bit at the top.

Use a toothbrush to clean round the gear lever
and in the switches on the dashboard.

Car a bit smelly?
    Freshen it up with a sheet of fabric
    conditioner placed under the seats.

Bikes and Bicycles

'Mind my bike'
Jack Warner

Clean the chain and cog system regularly
    – it will cost a few pennies, but will save
    a fortune in maintenance and repairs in
    the long run.

Polish any metal and painted surfaces
    with household wax to stop rust.

To get rid of rust from bicycle wheel rims,
    put some emery paper between the brake
    blocks. Turn the pedals and lightly apply
    the brakes.

Keep chrome looking shiny

– polish with a little bicarbonate of soda on a damp cloth. Rinse off and dry the chrome.

If you get bike oil on your clothes,

rub the stain with washing-up liquid and then wash as normal.

Tar and oil stains can be removed with toothpaste.

Keep a visor-wipe handy

– cut a tennis ball in half and tie it round the handle. It makes a great place to store a damp sponge, which you can use to keep your visor clean.

PREVENTION IS BETTER THAN CURE

. . . .

'They say hard work never hurt anybody,
but I figure why take the chance.'
Ronald Reagan

If your freezer is kept in the garage,
polish the outside of the cabinet with wax. This prevents it from being affected by damp, mould or rust.

To cut down on static
put a few drops of fabric conditioner in to some water and wipe down the front of your TV.

Wipe bathroom mirrors
with some washing-up liquid on a cloth – this will reduce condensation.

Or, try wiping with a baby wipe
and buff with kitchen paper towel for an effortless shine.

Prevent rusty rings in your bathroom.
Paint the bottom of aerosol cans with clear nail varnish.

If your acrylic bath gets scratched,
try rubbing the scratches with silver polish.

Keep flies away

– place fresh mint on the kitchen windowsill.

Stop dried pampas grass from disintegrating

– spray hair lacquer on so it holds its shape.

To prevent limescale build up,

clean your shower heads at least every three months.

Prevent bacteria from building up in your garden hose

– don't leave it lying around in the sun. The bacteria can breed very quickly.

To avoid wax on your tablecloths,

put a beer mat under the candles.

To keep clean when you are doing dirty work,

wear an old dustbin liner. It's easy to throw away each day.

Make your life easier

– put some washing-up liquid in the children's paint because it helps it to come out of their clothes when they are being washed.

To make non-dribbly paint,

mix it with wallpaper paste (but not one that has an anti-fungus agent in it) and it won't end up all over the place.

Prevent that lingering fish smell on plates

by putting a tablespoon of vinegar in the washing-up water.

Make your own protective castor mats

from the lids of coffee jars. Just slide under the castor to protect the pile of the carpet.

Keep your waste disposal unit smelling sweet by grating citrus rind into it.

Or use the discarded baking soda after it has finished absorbing odours in the refrigerator.

After cleaning cast iron,
while the pan is still warm, wipe with
a piece of wax paper to prevent rusting.
Or, when clean, rub a small amount of
vegetable oil on the inside to keep it
seasoned.

**Steel-wool pads won't get rusty if you throw
them in a plastic bag and store in the freezer.**

To prevent mildew forming in your fridge,
wipe with vinegar.

**To prevent mildew from forming on new
shower curtains,**
soak in salt water before hanging for the
first time.

When shampooing carpets,
put small plastic bags or glass jars around
furniture legs to prevent rust stains from
forming.

Wooden floors look lovely
and needn't be hard to maintain. The
trick is not to use too much polish – it

just traps more dirt. So, only use polish
every few months.

The bristles on your new broom

will last much longer if you dip the
broom head in salted water before you
use it. (This will only work on real
bristles though.)

Stop your vacuum cleaner from picking up metal pins and clips

by taping a magnet to the front of the
cleaner or the outside of the tube so they
don't get into the dust bag and damage it.

To prevent the smell of cigarette smoke from lingering,

put a small bowl of vinegar in the corner
of the room. Cover the bowl with cling
film and pierce it several times – then
you won't get vinegar everywhere if the
bowl is knocked over.

Prevent cigarette butts from smouldering.

Line your ash-trays with bicarbonate of
soda.

If you are drilling a hole for a curtain pole,
> vacuum up the dust at the same time to
> prevent it from getting everywhere or
> spoiling your new curtains.

Playing-cards can look pretty tatty,
> so after cleaning, dust them over with
> some talc to prevent further grimy
> marks.

**To prevent the bottom of a bathroom pull
cord becoming discoloured,**
> place the casing from a clear ballpoint
> pen over the 'pulling' end.

**To prevent mildew from forming in your
bathroom,**
> fill a small flat box with cat litter
> and place in the bottom of the tub –
> especially if you're going to be away
> for a long time. (Remember to keep
> the door shut if you've got cats!)

Stop windows from steaming up
> by putting glycerine or a little washing-
> up liquid in some water and wiping over
> the glass.

For easy-to-clean windowsills,
apply an ordinary bath sealant to the line where your sill joins the window frame. This preserves the life of the paintwork by stopping damp from getting under the paint.

Prevent rugs from getting worn and bald too quickly
– turn them regularly so that they get even wear.

Protect an unused piano from damp
by covering the working parts and keyboard with sheets of brown paper.

Before you start decorating,
rub your hands in petroleum jelly. You'll save time at the end of the day when the paint will wash out easily.

Always clear and prepare the area you are going to decorate,
remove as much as you can from the room and cover the furniture and floor with old sheets.

Don't get paint in your hair
— wear a shower cap.

Cover your spectacles with cling film
so that if you get paint on them, you can just peel the cling film away.

Avoid paint drips all over your hand –
wind a rubber band around the thick part of the paint brush handle to catch any drips.

When painting ceilings,
put the handle of the paint brush through an old sponge to catch any drips.

Don't spoil your newly painted wall with ugly ladder marks.
Pop a pair of clean socks over the ends of the ladder.

New paint can smell horrid for ages.
Stir in a couple of drops of vanilla essence to disguise nasty fumes.

Alternatively,

leave a cut onion in a recently painted room to get rid of the smell of paint.

Protect your walls when painting close-resting pipes

by sliding a sheet of cardboard down behind the pipes as you work.

Keep paint off odd shapes

such as taps or doorknobs by covering them with kitchen foil.

Keep a pair of shoes or slippers outside the room you are decorating.

Then you'll have something to change into if you need to go outside and you won't walk paint all over the house.

Stains are best treated immediately

– keep some diluted carpet shampoo ready in an old washing-up bottle so that when disaster strikes, you can act at once.

After washing your baking trays,

> put them back into the oven while its still
> warm – to prevent them from going rusty.

**Wrap fish, poultry, vegetables and hot
sandwiches,**

> especially bacon, in white kitchen paper
> towels when you microwave them. It
> will keep the oven clean from grease and
> moisture – they also absorb excess fat
> from the food so you don't eat it!

**When making pastry or cooking anything
messy**

> – keep a polythene bag beside you, so
> that if the phone rings you can pop your
> hand inside the bag and pick up the phone
> without making it sticky.

**To scoop the seeds out of a melon without
making a mess,**

> place your hand inside a plastic bag. When
> your hand is full of seeds, slip off the bag
> while turning it inside out.

Place individual sheets of fabric conditioner

> into empty luggage to prevent musty
> smells.

INDEX